Includes DVD of Sample Film Clips!

PICTUREYOURSELF
Directing a Movie

Step-by-Step Instruction
for Creating Short Films and More

Eric Nicholas

COURSE TECHNOLOGY
CENGAGE Learning™

Picture Yourself Directing a Movie
Eric Nicholas

Publisher and General Manager,
Course Technology PTR: Stacy L. Hiquet

Associate Director of Marketing: Sarah Panella

Manager of Editorial Services: Heather Talbot

Marketing Manager: Mark Hughes

Acquisitions Editor: Megan Belanger

Project Editor: Jenny Davidson

PTR Editorial Services Coordinator: Erin Johnson

Interior Layout: Shawn Morningstar

Cover Designer: Mike Tanamachi

DVD-ROM Producer: Brandon Penticuff

Indexer: Katherine Stimson

Proofreader: Kim Benbow

For product information and technology assistance, contact us at

Cengage Learning Customer and Sales Support,
1-800-354-9706

For permission to use material from this text or product, submit all requests online at
cengage.com/permissions

Further permissions questions can be emailed to
permissionrequest@cengage.com

Library of Congress Control Number: 2008923825
ISBN-13: 978-1-59863-489-1
ISBN-10: 1-59863-489-5

Course Technology
25 Thomson Place
Boston, MA 02210
USA

Cengage Learning is a leading provider of customized learning solutions with office locations around the globe, including Singapore, the United Kingdom, Australia, Mexico, Brazil, and Japan. Locate your local office at:
international.cengage.com/region

Cengage Learning products are represented in Canada by Nelson Education, Ltd.

For your lifelong learning solutions, visit **courseptr.com**
Visit our corporate website at **cengage.com**

Printed in the United States of America
1 2 3 4 5 6 7 11 10 09 08

This is for Martina, who knows why.
Boy, does she.

About the Author

Los Angeles screenwriter and director, ERIC NICHOLAS, is a graduate of the University of Southern California's prestigious School of Cinema-Television. Over the past ten years, he has worked for some of the top production companies in Hollywood, including Warner Bros.-based Alcon Entertainment (producers of the hit films *Insomnia* and *The Sisterhood of the Traveling Pants*) and Sony-based Escape Artists, where his script *Diary* is currently set up with Jennifer Aniston attached to star.

In 2005, Nicholas wrote and directed the psychological thriller *Alone with Her*, starring Colin Hanks (son of Tom). The movie premiered at the 2006 Tribeca Film Festival in New York City, where it was picked up for worldwide distribution by IFC Films and The Weinstein Company. The movie was released in 2007 to excellent reviews, including raves by the L.A. Times, New York Post, and Entertainment Weekly. Nicholas will next be directing the $12 million action-thriller *The Weaker Sex* (which he also wrote) in late 2008.

Table of Contents

Introduction

THIS BOOK IS AIMED at the beginner, someone who has circled the idea of directing a film or video for some time and perhaps even made a few home movies, but has never actually developed, organized, and shot dramatic fiction using real actors. The primary reason I chose to write this book is there are very few "roadmaps" out there for amateur directors who don't have the time or resources to attend film school, and have found instruction books on directing too complex and/or focused on technology.

This book steers clear of the "technical" aspects of directing because:

- ▶ There are already hundreds of books out there covering the "tech side" in exhaustive detai—what cameras to buy, their features, how to operate them, types of lighting set ups, editing software, and so forth. Don't get me wrong, these books definitely have their place, but they tend to confuse, overwhelm, and even discourage novice filmmakers. Further, they often cloud or ignore altogether what is truly important in making dramatic films—which I'll get to in a moment.

- ▶ Technology is constantly changing and improving, thus rendering many technically oriented directing books obsolete within a few months of their release. Consider, for example, the explosion of high-definition cameras in the last few years. In 2000, very few feature films were being shot on high def and they tended to be low-budget "indies" that couldn't afford to shoot on 35mm. Today, many big-budget Hollywood movies shoot on high def, given its huge advances in quality.

- ▶ The most important elements of a successful movie are story and performance. Consider any of your favorite films. Imagine them with ham-fisted dialogue, ridiculous plot twists, and horrible actors. Not so great anymore, huh? Now imagine them as they really are, but with a few scenes underlit or with some rough patches of sound. Not such a big deal, right? Of course, sound and picture quality are important to a movie, but when compared to story and performance, they don't hold a candle. The best directors in the world are served by script and acting. It's that simple.

This book honors these facts and gets you off on the right foot, focusing on what really matters. Now, obviously, I can't tell you how to be a great director. No one can. I can only teach you the fundamental principles of directing, especially on a low budget, which I believe once learned, will free your talent.

In addition to reading my book, I urge you to learn everything you can about filmmaking from other sources. Watch movies, good and bad, then watch them again and again. Concentrate on what makes them live and die. Study their story structure, camera work, acting, lighting, sound design. Make notes. Read the technical books when you feel ready. Also, read about film theory and history. Most important, close your eyes and imagine—stories, characters, images. Directing is turning these things, and more, into reality.

The Script—

Your First Priority

THE SCRIPT IS THE MOST IMPORTANT part of your movie. It's the foundation on which everything is built: acting, cinematic style, locations, audience reaction. . . everything. You can't make a great movie without a great script. It's that simple. And as a novice director, without the icing of big budget special effects and movie stars, your story, characters, and dialogue will be on full display for all to see. If they suck, there's no hiding it. On the other hand, if your script is well-written, without all the Hollywood noise and flash, your movie will truly shine. Just look at your favorite low-budget indie flicks. They all share great stories, great characters, great dialogue. Always remember, it costs virtually nothing to write a great script, and yet it's the most important thing in the success of your movie. I urge you to take advantage of this fact and bust your hump to make sure your screenplay is nothing less than stellar *before* you start shooting.

How to Get One

THERE ARE THREE WAYS to get a great script: write it yourself, purchase it, or hire someone to write it for you. As an amateur filmmaker, you're probably not in a position to buy a screenplay or hire a professional to write one for you. However, if you're lucky enough to discover a great script and the owner is willing to sell it to you for a song, you can find dozens of books out there on how to properly purchase a script. Same goes for how to hire and work with a writer.

Chances are, you will be penning the script yourself while getting input and feedback from your peers, friends, and family. As a new writer, your first order of business is to educate yourself on what makes a good story. Read every screenwriting how-to book you can get your hands on. Of particular importance is learning story structure, which I will cover later in this chapter. Also, attend some screenwriting workshops or seminars if you can; whatever is available in your area. And finally, read finished screenplays—lots of them—until you can instinctively tell the difference between good writing and bad. The scripts for almost all of your favorite movies are available online for free, so dive right in. Then get to work.

My two favorite sites for free movie scripts are:

1. JO BLO'S MOVIE SCRIPTS
http://www.joblo.com/moviescripts.php

2. DREW'S SCRIPT-O-RAMA
http://www.script-o-rama.com/table.shtml

To familiarize yourself with good screenwriting, I strongly recommend that you read the following classics:

1. *Chinatown* by Robert Towne
2. *Rocky* by Sylvester Stallone
3. *The Silence of the Lambs* by Ted Tally
4. *Pulp Fiction* by Quentin Tarantino
5. *The Shawshank Redemption* by Frank Darabont
6. *Platoon* by Oliver Stone
7. *Being John Malkovich* by Charlie Kaufman
8. *Schindler's List* by Steven Zaillian
9. *American Beauty* by Alan Ball
10. *Back to the Future* by Robert Zemeckis and Bob Gale

Ideas

SINCE YOU LIKELY WON'T be selling your movie idea to investors, studios, and ticket buyers, you can afford to indulge yourself creatively much more than professional movie directors who must always bow to the fact that their films are, first and foremost, marketing products—movies that appeal to the widest possible audience in order to justify their massive budgets. These movies tend to be simple, easy to digest, and are usually filled with empty spectacle. Now, don't get me wrong, I love big Hollywood popcorn flicks as much as the next guy, and I'm not suggesting that you make an esoteric art film that virtually no one can understand or enjoy. Movies are audience driven, made for the many, not the few. I'm simply pointing out that you're in a position to take creative risks with your movie, so don't squander this opportunity. At the same time, strive to clearly communicate with your audience and entertain them.

Here are a few key questions you should ask yourself when brainstorming a movie concept:

- ▶ **What message or theme am I passionate about?**
- ▶ **What kind of story and characters will get people interested in my message/theme?**
- ▶ **What will make my movie stand apart from all the others?**

If you don't have a great idea already in mind, do some exploring to spark your imagination—read books, magazine articles, edgy websites, dream, listen to songs, whatever it takes, until you're inspired.

Story Structure

EVERY MOVIE, REGARDLESS of its length, needs a beginning, middle, and end. In script talk, this is referred to as the three-act structure, which has been around since the ancient Greeks. Story structure is not a magic formula; it's just basic drama. Again, there are countless books available on this subject, but most of them apply to feature-length movies and may give you much more information than you really need at this stage.

Basically, your script should have three underlying sections called *acts*, as shown in Figure 1.1.

Act I introduces:

▶ **The main character(s)**

▶ **Where and when the story takes place**

▶ **An incident or dilemma that forces your central character (protagonist) to take action**

▶ **The manner in which your protagonist sets out to achieve his/her goal**

The dilemma or inciting incident that your protagonist faces in the first act is often referred to as "the hook" of your movie, and it must be intriguing enough to hold your audience's interest throughout. Your main job in Act I is to grab your audience.

Figure 1.1

Beginning Act I	Middle Act II	End Act III
Setup Consists of about 25% of your script	Confrontation About 50% of your script	Resolution About 25% of your script

In Act II, you need to create obstacles that prevent your main character from solving his dilemma. These obstacles usually come from the antagonist ("the bad guy") of your story. It's very important that these obstacles become more and more difficult for your protagonist as Act II progresses, so your audience feels an escalation to the drama. This applies to any story dilemma, whether it's subtle or in-your-face. A character pursuing the love of his life in a romantic comedy needs to face obstacles as much as a character fighting flesh-eating zombies in a horror movie.

In Act III, your story should come to a resolution in the most dramatic fashion possible. Your protagonist should face his greatest challenge at a peak of physical or emotional action—and either succeed or fail.

Using a romantic comedy as a model, the three-act structure can be simply summarized as follows:

Act I: Boy meets girl and gets girl.

Act II: Boy loses girl.

Act III: Boy gets girl back.

Even though the boy gets the girl in Act I, the possibility of losing her should be in the air throughout the act. In Act II, the relationship starts to come apart as the antagonist runs interference and causes problems. The romance then crumbles, with the antagonist apparently the victor. But by the end of Act II, the boy will resolve to win his girl back and defeat his foe. In Act III, the boy puts his plan into action and gets his girl back. Figure 1.2 shows a graphic representation of this scenario.

Figure 1.2

Beginning Act I	Middle Act II	End Act III
Setup Boy meets girl and gets girl. At the end of this act a significant Turning Point occurs, which moves the drama in a new direction. In this case, perhaps the antagonist shows up and presents serious competition for the girl's affections.	**Confrontation** Boy loses girl. The antagonist runs interference, causing problems, and lures the girl away from the boy. At the end of this act, it appears that the boy has lost, but he resolves to win the girl back (second Turning Point) and defeat the antagonist – ideally, with a new, clever plan.	**Resolution** Boy gets girl back. The boy puts his plan into action and, though it doesn't go perfectly, he wins the girl back in the end and defeats the antagonist.

Story Outline

PERSONALLY, I FIND IT CRUCIAL to outline my story before going "in script." I usually do this in bullet form, detailing every scene in each act. Figure 1.3 shows the Act I story outline for an original screenplay of mine titled, *Academic Misconduct*.

Outlining will help you develop the cause and effect of your story, or the actions and reactions, as well as the characters. It will also help you clarify structure and serve as a blueprint on which you can build all the details of your story. Most important, it will let you see your film as a whole in just a few pages, allowing you to spot any problem areas. If you try to develop your story and characters "in script," you're going to have a lot of false starts and hit a lot of dead ends after investing many hours, if not days, of hard work. You may even discover that your script is a total mess after finishing the whole thing—and have to start from scratch! Don't go down that road.

A solid outline will free your creativity when you're writing the script because you'll know exactly where you're going. You'll have figured out your story, characters, and structure, so you'll be able to focus your heart and mind on the drama and dialogue in each scene. You'll be able to let your imagination soar—while remaining *in control*.

Once you're in script, you may find that things are changing from what you originally imagined in your outline. Don't let this frighten you; embrace it. Writing a story is a journey of discovery and you want your script to evolve into something deep and rich. The story outline simply provides you with a roadmap. It should give you confidence that you know where you're going.

Figure 1.3

ACT I

- Tommy stands in the restroom, fighting off a major anxiety attack.
- Tommy and Steve walk down the school corridor, quickly going over their strategy. Tommy very nervous, uncertain.
- Tommy and Steve ask teacher's assistant, Beth, to help them cheat by getting a copy of the exam. She agrees for a hefty price.
- Tommy and Steve in their dormitory hallway. Steve happy; Tommy torn.
- In their dorm room, Steve playfights with Tommy until Tommy loosens up and accepts what they're doing. Knock at the door interrupts. Sandra, Tommy's long-time girlfriend. Steve checks phone messages as Sandra tells Tommy about new dinner plans. Steve curses as he gets off the phone, has to go to work, leaves. Sandra indicates that she doesn't like Steve.
- Surprise birthday party for Tommy at fancy restaurant (Sandra organized it). Tommy's parents in attendance along with friends, close family. More backstory revealed. Dad makes a speech indicating his sky-high expectations for Tommy. Tommy clearly affected.
- 3 weeks later. Exam season. Tommy and Steve studying hard. Beth calls to confirm she got a copy of the exam. Will give it to them on Sunday at 2pm.
- Sunday. Tommy and Steve get Beth's money from ATM. Walk to Beth's sorority house in high spirits.
- They arrive to discover that the exam was stolen from Beth's room in a home robbery last night. They angrily confront Beth. She tells them there's nothing she can do and walks out on them, leaving them high and dry.

Character

I CAN'T EMPHASIZE ENOUGH the importance of fresh, dimensional characters. Think about your favorite movies; what do you remember most, the interesting characters you met or the plot details? I'm willing to bet it was the characters. Since you are making an independent film and have unlimited creative freedom, it's imperative that you create striking and unique characters. Not only is this more exciting to your audience, but it will make your film stand out from typical (and predictable) Hollywood fare. So resist the clichés and surprise your audience with new, memorable characters.

Before you start writing your script, I strongly suggest that you create a personal history for each main character. Include as much detail as possible—from their "givens," such as age, sex, appearance, etc., to deeper, more action-oriented details like what they want, what's stopping them, and how they overcome their obstacles. These personal histories will allow you to truly *know* your characters and help you determine what they do and say at every step. I have included a sample character profile from one of my recent movies in Figure 1.4.

Since a character's true nature is revealed through conflict, it's important that you pit your protagonist against the strongest antagonist you can dream up. Someone with completely opposing goals. The resulting collision will create great drama. Strong villains are often crucial to successful stories.

In Hollywood, screenplay development executives often insist that your main character be sympathetic—in other words, a good person that the audience will like and root for. There is some truth to this idea, but if your aim is to make a great independent film, I strongly suggest that you rise above two-dimensional lily-white characters and go for something edgy and dangerous. You can even make your protagonist a despicable SOB with no redeeming qualities. Why not? If he's interesting, the audience will be glued to his every move and word. However, if you're concerned that people will hate him and tune out, give him just a hint of something we can relate to: a sense of humor, a vague soft side, or a character flaw such as jealousy, pride, or cowardice. It's these flaws that make us human, after all—and intriguing.

A final note on your main characters: ideally, they experience a change over the course of the story; they evolve or grow in some way. These changes can be extreme or subtle—a cynical young woman opening her heart to love again, or a violent racist gaining just an inch of tolerance and understanding. This "character arc" is usually quite satisfying to an audience, but whether you use it or not will depend on the nature of your story and, to a large extent, on your film's length. Obviously, a five-minute short film does not lend itself well to character development, but a 20-minute film (or longer) does.

Figure 1.4

Paul Hunter

Born to middle-class parents in a small town in eastern Oregon. When he was six, his alcoholic father abandoned the family, leaving Paul with a neurotic mother who was forced to work two jobs in order to make ends meet.

Skinny and socially awkward as a kid, he was constantly picked on. Terrible at sports. Few friends. Spent considerable time alone, watching TV, movies, reading: the beginnings of a powerful fantasy life.

In high school, despite his efforts to fit in, he was regarded as something of an oddball—still very thin, insecure, shabby clothes, bad acne. Often ridiculed. Suffered periods of deep depression. Found refuge in more TV, computers, plus a growing interest in pornography.

In his late teens, he developed physically into a decent looking kid, but by this time his feelings of insignificance and inadequacy were fully entrenched, a permanent part of his personality. Rarely dated. Graduated still a virgin.

Studied computer science at Oregon State University. Very lonely there, until he met a young woman in his sophomore year. They became friends and dated a few times, but ultimately she found him too insecure and needy and pulled away.

Wounded, he continued to pursue her, repeatedly calling her, sending gifts, showing up at her door, etc. He desperately hoped that he just had to show her how much he loved her and that would be enough to win her back. Instead, her frustration boiled over and she threatened to report him to the police.

Humiliated, he verbally (and profanely) lashed out at her, forever ending their relationship (note: studies show that an intense narcissistic reaction to rejection and loss is common with this type of character. The man defends himself against intense feelings of humiliation, shame, and sadness by narcissistic rage, during which he starts devaluing – and sometimes torturing – his love object. This will obviously come into play with Holly.)

A deep depression followed, during which he failed several of his courses. Dropped out of college in his junior year. Unable to bear moving back home, he drifted from town to town for a couple of years, holding down various menial jobs, finally landing in L.A., where he managed to lie his way into a sales job with a small publishing house.

As the movie opens, Paul is in the red zone of his loneliness and sexual frustration. He is socially withdrawn and completely isolated from real life, at home only in the world of movies, TV, and the Internet. He has never had a close relationship with a woman, never had sex, and has no immediate prospects of either. His "outlets" consist solely of pornography (to which he is now addicted) and fledgling voyeurism.

Upon finding Holly, he is prepared to do anything to win her over, desperate for intimacy... all personal morality out the window, his entire identity buried and reinvented.

He believes that Holly is his destiny. He sees the two of them as halves of the same whole, incomplete without each other. Pursuing her becomes his full-time obsession, providing meaning in a life that previously had none.

Dialogue

As I mentioned in the last section, who a character is determines what he says and how he says it. Of course, how your character is feeling at any given moment also influences what comes out of his mouth. I urge you to concentrate on these factors whenever you're writing character dialogue or action. Who is this person? What's his past? His future? How does he intend to get there? Eventually, you'll know these answers instinctively and find it quite easy (and exciting) to slip into each character's skin. You'll know their souls.

If there's one cardinal rule of writing dialogue it's *never be on-the-nose*. There's nothing more painful than hearing a character say exactly what's on his mind—like, "I have a fear of commitment because my parents abandoned me as a child." Who, in real life, speaks that way? No one. Important character issues are almost always hinted at, or revealed through behavior. In fact, it's often what we don't say that has the greatest impact—a simple look or physical reaction. On that note, always try to show, not tell, since you're working in a visual medium. Reveal information with images and action as much as possible.

Once you've put your dialogue to paper, a valuable test of its quality is to read it out loud. Words that you thought were positively brilliant at your computer can often sound downright ridiculous when actually spoken. For that reason, it's very important to rehearse your script before shooting (ideally, with actors) and change whatever dialogue that doesn't sound right.

Screenplay Format

OKAY, SO YOU'VE OUTLINED your story and developed your characters. Now, you're ready to pour it all into a properly formatted screenplay. The main reason to format your script is to get an idea of how long your film is going to be—i.e., it's running time. Roughly speaking, one formatted page equals one minute of screen time.

Believe it or not, formatting a script is pretty simple. In fact, virtually your entire script will involve only four elements: Scene Headings, Action, Character Names, and Dialogue. Once you've learned how to format these basic building blocks, you're good to go.

Scene headings appear at the beginning of a new scene and tell us where and when the scene is taking place. They are always capitalized and look like this:

INT. OFFICE – NIGHT

Or this:

EXT. DESERT – DAY

INT. is short for Interior (indoors) and EXT. is short for Exterior (outdoors). Next is where the scene takes place. Try to make these short, like JOE'S BEDROOM or SOCCER FIELD. Finally, there is the time. Usually, just DAY or NIGHT, but if you need to be as specific as 2:23 P.M. (because somebody's getting shot at 2:24 P.M.) then by all means type it in. Remember, you need a new scene heading every time there's a change in time, location, or both.

Action describes what's happening on the screen and which characters, if any, are involved, as shown in Figure 1.5.

As you can see, action follows the standard rules of capitalization. It's written in the present tense and single-spaced.

Figure 1.5

```
INT. DORM ROOM — NIGHT

Tommy sits at his desk,
hunched over some textbooks,
studying hard.  His tense,
twitching eyes devouring
information, his pen
quickly scrawling key terms,
passages.
```

Character names always appear above dialogue and, obviously, indicate who is speaking. They are always in caps, whereas dialogue is not; it is single-spaced and follows the standard rules of capitalization like your action (see Figure 1.6).

Figure 1.7 shows how all four elements come together.

And that's it. You're ready to go "in script." There are many little formatting variations to the above elements, but instead of clouding your mind with them, I suggest you take look at the screenplay sample I've included in Appendix B.

Figure 1.6

```
          TOMMY
I'm going home now and if you
follow me there's gonna be
trouble.
```

Figure 1.7

```
EXT. SCHOOL BUILDING — DAY

Tommy exits the building and finds Steve waiting for him,
suppressing a smirk.  They share a look — and Steve wraps
his arms around Tommy, bursting with joy.

               STEVE
     We did it!
```

You should also review as many finished, well-written screenplays as you can. As I've said, they're available for free online and are incredibly instructive—not only in terms of formatting but in terms of good screenwriting.

I have included a formatted script page in Figure 1.8 to guide you through formatting.

As for the proper font, margins, and spacing, this is how it lays out:

You will be writing on letter-sized paper (8.5 x 11 inches). Always in Courier font, 12 point, 10 pitch. Page margins are

Left: 1.5 inches

Right: 1 inch

Top: 1 inch

Bottom: 1 inch

Scene headings: left margin 1.5 inches

Action: left margin 1.5 inches

Character name: left margin 3.7 inches

Dialog: left margin 2.5 inches, right margin 2.5 inches

Figure 1.8

INT. TOMMY AND STEVE'S DORM ROOM - DAY

For the truly ambitious, a pressure-cooker season of sleepless nights, twisted backs, and debilitating stress.

Tommy sits at his desk, hunched over some books, studying hard. Tense, twitching eyes devouring information, pen quickly scrawling key terms, passages.

SLOWLY MOVING across the room, we find Steve at his desk in identical form, beads of perspiration collecting on his forehead.

The phone RINGS suddenly! Steve SNATCHES the receiver.

>   STEVE
>   (quiet, icy)
>   Hello... Yeah...What's the
>   verdict?

A long silence as he listens. Tommy lifts his head.

>   STEVE
>   (continuing)
>   Any backup?... Better make a hard
>   copy ASAP, just in case... Right...
>   Sounds good... OK, later.

He hangs up. Pauses.

>   STEVE
>   She got it.

>   TOMMY
>   Any problems?

>   STEVE
>   Zero. Next Sunday, two o'clock.

Tommy smiles, relieved. Returns to his studies.

INT. STUDENT CENTER - NEXT SUNDAY - DAY

AN ATM coughs out a wad of cash for Tommy. He hands the bills to Steve who slips them in an envelope. Smirks.

Some Low-Budget Rules

SINCE YOU ACTUALLY WANT to produce the script you write and have a very low budget (I assume), here are some general guidelines to follow when writing:

1. Limit the number of your locations. Every move to a new location costs time—and time is money in film production. The fewer locations you have, the better.

2. Pay nothing (or next to nothing) for your locations and make sure they're easily accessible. Using your own house, cottage, backyard, etc. is the best way to go, as you can shoot 24/7, move furniture (even break things!) without interference from some irate owner.

3. Keep your cast small. It doesn't matter if your actors are working for free. You still have to feed them, schedule them, keep them comfortable between shots, and probably buy them wardrobe. Trust me, it adds up.

4. Avoid expensive costumes, props, and set dressings, which are often required in period pieces, science-fiction films, etc.

5. Obviously, avoid complicated stunts like dangerous falls, swordplay, fighting, etc. You won't be able to afford a professional stunt person, and if one of your cast tries a stunt and gets seriously injured, you'll never forgive yourself.

6. Steer clear of special effects. You can probably afford some blank gunshots and gory makeup (as shown in Figures 1.9 and 1.10) but anything more—fires, explosions, car crashes—and you're asking for trouble.

7. Don't write any scenes that require shooting in extreme weather conditions (heavy rain, snow, etc.). You can't afford to artificially create extreme weather and shooting in the real thing is very tough. It will slow you down to a crawl, cause all sorts of continuity problems, and may even damage your equipment.

8. Always strive for creative solutions to your budget constraints. For example, the *sounds* of an expensive car crash, coupled with someone's horrified reaction shot, can be quite impactful if done skillfully.

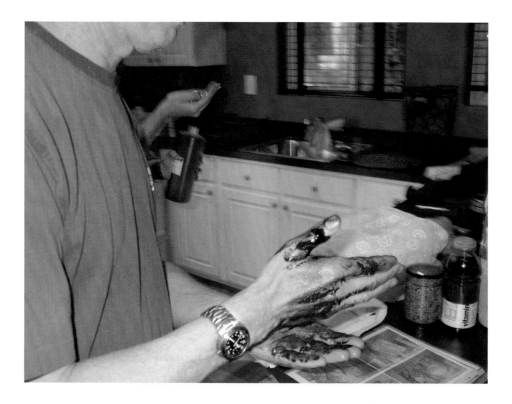

Figures 1.9 and 1.10
Shooting in black and white on my first feature, *River Rats*, we were able to use simple chocolate syrup to simulate blood.

Summary

In summary, be sure to do the following when it comes to your screenplay:

▶ **Learn story structure.**

▶ **Attend a screenwriting workshop or seminar, if you can.**

▶ **Read as many quality screenplays as possible.**

▶ **Latch onto a story idea/theme that excites you and that you're confident will interest audiences.**

▶ **Outline your entire story in bullet form before starting your script. The more detail the better.**

▶ **Make sure all your characters are unique, interesting, and fully fleshed out.**

▶ **Make sure your dialogue is fresh and clever. Read it out loud and rehearse it until you're completely satisfied it's the best it can be.**

▶ **Learn basic screenplay format.**

▶ **Keep your budget in mind when writing your script. Be realistic.**

Getting Ready to
Shoot

TO FIGURE OUT HOW MUCH your film is going to cost to make, you need a finished script. Now that you have one, you can prepare a realistic budget. Given your circumstances, your budget will be very small: a few thousand bucks at most, and probably much less. Hopefully, your available resources were at the forefront of your mind while you were writing the script and you haven't gotten in over your head. In any event, the following process will tell you very quickly whether you can afford to shoot what you wrote.

Scheduling

YOUR FIRST STEP IS TO SET a timetable for your movie, covering pre-production through post-production. A sample calendar for a micro-budget movie looks something like this:

Week 1: Start hiring crew members and begin casting.

Week 2: Scout locations, secure equipment and props, and continue casting and securing crew positions.

Week 3: Complete casting and crewing, start rehearsals, and lock down your locations.

Week 4: Production.

Week 5: Start editing your rough cut.

Week 6: Edit picture and sound, tighten your cut.

Week 7: Add/compose music.

Week 8: Complete your final cut.

I'll discuss these elements in more detail throughout the rest of this book, but for now let's move on to "breaking down" your script into a shooting schedule. Breaking down a screenplay is actually quite simple. Just divide the script into scenes and note the location, required actors, props you will need, etc. (see Figure 2.1):

Of course, also make any notes that you feel are important to the shoot. From the breakdown, you'll get an idea of how many shooting days are required to complete your film. How much money you have will be an important factor at this point, as will the style in which you plan to shoot your movie and the availability of your actors, crew, and equipment. You may realize that the only way to make your film is to shoot on weekends, so that your cast and crew (who have real jobs) are available, and your equipment and locations can be secured for little or no money.

Just like studio pictures, you will be shooting all your scenes at a particular location at the same time, no matter where they appear in the script. This "shooting out of sequence" will minimize your travel between locations and save you oceans of time (and cash!). Also, organize your schedule so that you're using any expensive rental equipment, props, actors, locations, etc. for the minimum number of days.

A final tip before you shoot: be prepared! Create detailed shot lists and storyboards (covered in Chapter 6) as early as possible, knowing exactly what you want from top to bottom—shots, camera moves, actor positions, props, wardrobe, etc. Do everything you can to use the minimum amount of camera setups in order to get the maximum number of shots. Moving equipment, heavy props, etc. and relighting everything for a new setup can suck up valuable hours.

Figure 2.1

Script Breakdown Sheet

Production Company: _____

Production Title: _____

Date: _____

Breakdown Page: _____

Page Count: _____

| _____ | _____ | _____ |
| Scene Number | Scene Name | Interior or Exterior |

CAST	STUNTS	EXTRAS
SPECIAL EFFECTS	**PROPS**	**VEHICLES/ANIMALS**
WARDROBE	**MAKEUP/HAIR**	**SPECIAL EQUIPMENT**
PRODUCTION NOTES		

Budget

GIVEN YOUR LIMITED FUNDS, it's crucial that you plan carefully how you're going to spend your money. Be anal. Be obsessive-compulsive. Account for every penny. Make some allowances for unexpected delays/problems. Most important, allow yourself time to shop for bargains.

Your best guidance at this point is your fellow filmmakers, people who have made movies for budgets similar to yours. Pick their brains when it comes to hiring crew and securing equipment. Their recommendations can save you considerable time and money.

If you don't know such people, call up a local film/TV producer and ask him for advice, names, contact numbers. Your success depends largely on your willingness to ask for help, to bargain and, sometimes, to beg. In fact, you (or someone on your team) must be a master at haggling, bartering, and negotiating the best deals. Remember to always shop around. When potential equipment suppliers know you have options, their prices drop very quickly. As for the various quotes you get, never agree to prices on published rate cards. It's an unwritten rule in the film business that rate cards are inflated (sometimes grossly) and that you should never pay what's quoted.

When preparing official budgets, most professional filmmakers use industry software programs that include hundreds of line items—costs for the production manager, assistant directors, production design, grips, insurance, etc. Fortunately, your budget will be much simpler and probably contain only 20-30 line items. I'm confident you can prepare such a budget with nothing more than a pen and paper or a simple word processor/spreadsheet. Just list your line items on the left and their corresponding costs on the right, then total everything, as in Figure 2.2.

Many (if not most) of your line items will total $0, since you'll no doubt be working for free as the writer, director, producer, and probably editor. And your cast and crew will probably be working for nothing more than screen credit, meals, and maybe some gas money. The bulk of your costs at this level will be for camera, lighting and editing equipment, and film/videotape stock.

A final word of advice: take care of your cast and crew—especially if you're not paying them. Making a movie is hard, tedious work, and this reality sinks in very quickly for newcomers looking for a kick. It's imperative that you feed your people well, always respect them, and try to make the experience as enjoyable as possible. Otherwise, you may find no one shows up for work after Day One.

Figure 2.2

SAMPLE BUDGET

writer/director/producer	$X
cast	$X
extras	$X
cameraman	$X
production assistants	$X
sound recordist	$X
makeup and hair	$X
props	$X
wardrobe expenses	$X
location expenses	$X
equipment rental	$X
film/videotape stock	$X
meals	$X
miscellaneous expenses	$X
TOTAL PRODUCTION COSTS	$X
editor	$X
editing equipment	$X
composer/music	$X
TOTAL POST-PRODUCTION COSTS	$X
TOTAL BUDGET	**$X**

Paperwork

SINCE YOU'RE NOT making a big-budget feature that's going to be released all over the world by a major distributor, your paperwork only needs to cover a few things: equipment insurance, location releases, and actor releases. You can easily find free samples of all these forms online, but for your convenience I've attached some samples of my own (see Figures 2.3 and 2.4).

Equipment insurance covers you for damage to production items that you rent, such as camera and sound equipment, lighting, vehicles, expensive props, etc. Typically, the production house from which you're renting will provide you with insurance options before you take out any equipment.

A location release gives you official permission to use property that isn't your own for the purpose of shooting your movie. This permission includes the right to bring cast, crew, equipment, etc. onto the property. The release also typically holds the owner of the property harmless from any liability that you and your people may incur through accidents or damages to equipment.

Actor releases are necessary for all people who appear on camera and for everyone whose voice is heard. These releases give you the right to photograph/record your actors and exhibit the footage any way you see fit. Don't get lazy with these. Without actor releases you're extremely vulnerable to any on-screen individual coming out of the woodwork after your movie's shot and threatening all kinds of legal action if you show their face/voice on screen.

Figure 2.3

Sample Location Release Form

Gentlemen:

I (we) hereby grant to you, your successors, assigns and licensees, the right to photograph, reproduce, and use the exteriors and interiors of the premises located at _____, and to bring personnel and equipment onto the premises and remove same.

You may have possession of the premises on _____, 2008, and may continue in possession thereof until the completion of your proposed scenes and work on _____, 2008.

This is in connection with the motion picture tentatively entitled _____ and includes the right to use the photography in connection with the exhibition, advertising and promotion of the motion picture, in any manner whatsoever and at any time in any part of the world.

You agree to hold me (us) free from any claims for damage or injury arising during your occupancy of the premises and arising out of your negligence thereon, and to leave the premises in as good order and condition as when received by you, reasonable wear and tear, and use herein permitted excepted.

I (we) acknowledge that, in photographing the premises, you are not in any way depicting or portraying me (us) in the motion picture, either directly or indirectly. I (we) will not maintain against you any claim of any kind whatsoever, including, without limitation, those based upon invasion of privacy or other civil rights, defamation, libel or slander, in connection with the exercise of the permission herein granted.

I (we) represent that I (we) are the owner(s) and/or authorized representative(s) of the premises, and that I (we) have the authority to grant you the permission and rights herein granted, and that no one else's permission is required.

Dated: _____

Signature of Owner or Authorized Agent _____

Figure 2.4

Sample Actor Release Form

FOR VALUABLE CONSIDERATION, including the agreement to produce the motion picture currently entitled _____, I hereby irrevocably grant to XYZ Productions, its licensees, agents, successors and assigns, the right (but not the obligation), in perpetuity throughout the world, in all media, now or hereafter known, to use (in any manner it deems appropriate, and without limitation) in and in connection with the motion picture, by whatever means exhibited, advertised or exploited: my appearance in the motion picture, still photographs of me, recordings of my voice taken or made of me by it, any music sung or played by me, and my actual or fictitious name.

On my own behalf, and on behalf of my heirs, next of kin, executors, administrators, successors and assigns, I hereby release XYZ Productions, its agents, licensees, successors and assigns, from any and all claims, liabilities and damages arising out of the rights granted hereunder, or the exercise thereof.

Date_____

Signature_____

Locations

AT YOUR BUDGET LEVEL it doesn't make any sense to rent an expensive soundstage, build a set from scratch, or hassle yourself with obtaining official location permits (and paying through the nose for them) to shoot in busy public areas. I urge you to keep your locations simple and safe. The ideal, of course, is to shoot in your own home in a spot that requires little if any set dressing or construction. Other reasonable options include property owned by your close family and friends, your place of work, and any deserted or isolated area where there's virtually no chance of disturbing anyone.

When scouting locations, be sure to take many pictures so that no detail is overlooked or forgotten, and so that you can carefully review them later. Taking photos also allows you to capture any images that strike a chord with you, images that perhaps define the tone or style that you want for your movie. On my first feature, *River Rats*, I took many location photos that perfectly captured the cinematic style I was shooting for––dark and foreboding, a sense of desolation and decay (see Figures 2.5 to 2.10). These images allowed me to clearly communicate what I wanted to my cast and crew and also acted as inspiration throughout the shoot.

Figure 2.5

Figure 2.6

Figure 2.7

Figure 2.8

Figure 2.9

Figure 2.10

When scouting a location, here are a few important things to consider:

▶ Noise. **Is there a lot of traffic nearby, or other unwanted sounds? Excess noise can easily destroy your sound recordings.**

▶ Space. **Is there enough for your camera, lighting equipment, cast and crew? How big are the rooms, hallways, doorways? How low are the ceilings? Are there any difficult stairways to contend with? Is there space to feed your people, to store equipment? What about parking?**

▶ Power. **Can you use your location's power source? Is it easily accessible?**

Wardrobe and Makeup

WHEN IT COMES TO MAKEUP and wardrobe on a no-budget shoot, you need only remember three words: do it yourself! Actually, your cast will be doing it themselves—providing their own clothes and makeup, unless you were crazy enough to write a period piece or sci-fi thriller that requires pricey costumes (and locations, special effects, etc.).

Before shooting begins, set up a room or area where your actors can get dressed and put on their makeup in relative privacy (see Figures 2.11 and 2.12). All wardrobe, makeup, and props should be stored in this room for the duration of the shoot, so that everything is easily accessible and nothing gets lost.

Figure 2.11

Figure 2.12

Food

AS I MENTIONED EARLIER, it's crucial that you feed your cast and crew well, especially on a low-budget shoot. It's not just matter of consideration. Food is fuel. If you skimp on it, your movie is going to suffer tremendously. Assuming a shoot starts early in the morning and goes for 12 hours, you should plan to provide a balanced breakfast, lunch, and dinner to your cast and crew, along with a variety of snacks and beverages in between meals. To save money, you can buy and prepare much of this food yourself and/or have family friends help you out.

Figure 2.13
Signs of a happy, satiated cast and crew.

Equipment

HOPEFULLY, AS YOU PREPARE to shoot your film your need for stuff you don't already own will be very low; ideally, nonexistent. In any case, before you start renting or buying things, do a hard target search of every friend, family member, acquaintance, actor, crew member, etc. to see if they have what you're looking for. You can't afford to be bashful, so just steel yourself and ask around. In the end, if you find you still need to rent/buy then put your deal-making hat on and get to work.

Given your budget level, I'm assuming you already own a camera, probably a consumer digital camcorder as shown in Figures 2.14 and 2.15. If you don't own one, buy one! A good camera is the one piece of equipment a budding director should own. It will allow you to experiment and shoot anytime, anywhere. There are dozens of affordable, high-quality cameras on the market. Even High Definition camcorders are becoming affordable now, averaging about $1,000. If you don't have the coin for a camera, borrow one from somebody. Almost every Tom, Dick, and Harriet owns a camcorder these days. My point here is, when it comes to the camera, avoid having to rent one.

Figure 2.14

Figure 2.15

By the way, a dolly is a good piece of camera equipment to have on set—basically a little buggy/cart on which you mount your camera to allow smooth tracking shots. Since you can't afford to rent a professional dolly, simply buy or rent a wheelchair. Make sure it moves smoothly and quietly. You or your camera man will sit in it, aiming the camera, and someone else will push. If your location doesn't have a smooth floor surface, laying down some sheets of plywood should solve the problem.

When it comes to your lighting package, you have three choices: rent what you need (after shopping around, of course), borrow what you need (from crew/contacts), or improvise. For very little money, you can buy useful lighting equipment at just about any hardware store. For example, a sheet of polished metal can easily be used to reflect light (Figure 2.16), and a piece of black cardboard can be made into a "flag" to block light (Figure 2.17).

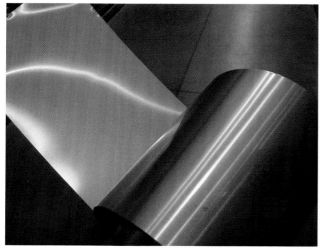

Figure 2.16

Figure 2.17

As for your actual lighting sources, a few high-wattage light bulbs (250 watts or more) will do the trick (Figure 2.18). Push yourself to be creative. It's the only way to make a movie in a cash crunch.

Figure 2.18

Some other equipment tips:

▶ Instead of renting a truck to transport/store your equipment, borrow one.

▶ If you're using a "sound guy," make sure he has his own gear so you can hire him as a package. Otherwise, use an external microphone that plugs into your camera's mic-in jack. That way you can record your actors from some distance.

▶ Stock up on expendables like batteries, tape, bulbs, etc.

▶ Don't rent your props, set dressing, or wardrobe from expensive studio departments or rental houses. Borrow them or buy them at discount stores, thrift shops, flea markets, and garage sales. Also, be sure to have duplicates of your important props, in case one gets damaged or lost.

▶ Finally, try to set aside a small contingency fund—cash that can be used to cover a surprise expense/emergency during production.

Summary

▶ Set a timetable for your movie.

▶ Break down your script to determine your shooting schedule.

▶ Be prepared—create all the necessary lists, storyboards, etc. so there's no wasted time on set.

▶ Prepare your budget.

▶ Talk to other low-budget filmmakers about where to get the best deals, and shop around on your own. Be creative.

▶ Make sure you've completed the necessary paperwork.

▶ Find shooting locations that you have free and easy access to, and that require little, if any, set construction/dressing.

▶ Have your cast provide their own wardrobe and do their own makeup.

▶ Don't skimp on food for your cast and crew. Food is fuel!

▶ Before buying or renting equipment, find out if someone you know has what you need. If you don't own a digital camcorder, buy one. Improvise whenever possible.

Casting

M ANY PEOPLE SAY THAT CASTING is 90% of
a director's job, and there is some truth to that
statement. No matter how great the other elements
of your film are, if the acting is poor, or if an actor is wrong
for a particular role, your movie will be crippled forever. In
my view, after the script, casting is the most crucial element
in filmmaking. You *have* to pick the right actors, whatever
it takes.

Developing Character Descriptions

BEFORE YOU CAN SEARCH for actors, you need basic descriptions of all your main characters, so that you can post/advertise them in the appropriate places (Internet, newspapers, local theaters, etc.). A few examples:

▶ Martina, late 30s. A high school beauty queen gone to seed. Divorced. Still living in the glory days of her past. Bitter that she'll never recapture them.

▶ Gary, 22, first year law student, handsome, driven. Determined to graduate at the top of his class in order to win the approval of his demanding father. Under extreme stress, often paralyzed by fear of failure.

▶ Jean, 69, widowed, struggling with rheumatoid arthritis. No close family around her, essentially a shut-in. Desperately lonely.

Thumbnail sketches like these compress a lot into a few sentences and allow the reader to make certain inferences about physical appearance, personal history, etc. In other words, these sketches encourage readers (especially actors) to open their imaginations and fill in the blanks themselves.

Looking for Talent

BIG-BUDGET FEATURE FILMS use the services of a casting director, a professional who brings to your attention the kind of actors you're looking for. They pre-screen performers, help conduct auditions, send you videotapes of top candidates, etc. Since a casting director is out of your price range, you will have to assume all of these responsibilities. The good news is, there are scores of talented performers out there desperate for experience and the chance to showcase themselves. All you have to do is find them. Here's how:

▶ **List your production in the acting trade papers**, like *Back Stage* (New York) and *Back Stage West* (Los Angeles). If you live outside these two cities, find some regional casting papers and place an ad. Describe your movie and the available roles in as much detail as possible. Be sure to mention that it's a non-union shoot and what you're paying, if anything (see Figure 3.1).

If there's no pay, explain what you are offering—and I urge you to offer *something*. No people are more important to the success of your film than the actors.

Treat them well. Even if you can only afford to pay them $10 or $20 per day, it'll go a long way for you. First, it'll distinguish your production from student films (which notoriously overwork everyone for zero pay and rarely result in anything good). Second, it will probably attract a bigger and better pool of actors, as even extremely low pay suggests professionalism. If you can't afford to pay anyone, I strongly suggest you offer free meals, a credit in the movie, a DVD of the finished film, and perhaps even gas money. Finally, be sure to mention in your ad that you're shooting a short and when your start date is.

▶ **Place ads in your local newspapers and magazines, and post online as well.** Any publication or website that gets the word out is fair game, including college and alternative papers, entertainment rags, Craigslist, etc. Some eye-catching headlines: "Actors Wanted," or "Casting Major Movie." Use your imagination and stir up a great response.

- ▶ **Post your ads wherever you feel actors hang out.** Some good bets are community theaters, drama schools, arts centers, and coffee shops. Since you're posting a hard copy of your ad, be sure it looks professional and enticing.

- ▶ **Pound the pavement and ask around for some recommendations.** Again, sniff out popular actor hang-outs and muster the courage to introduce yourself and your project. If you're polite and enthusiastic, you'll find that all kinds of people will step up and give you suggestions, including casting directors, acting teachers, agents, managers, film students, secretaries, etc. Don't be shy but always be honest about your project and your level of experience. If you intentionally misrepresent your film as something bigger and better than it actually is, you're going to burn a lot of bridges down the road and be on the receiving end of walk-outs, cursing, and possibly even threats.

I'm not going to lie to you—with a rock-bottom budget, you're going to have to work hard. Great actors for your film are out there, but you're going to need ingenuity and diligence to snag them. Just never forget that your film's credibility *depends* on a believable human presence onscreen.

Figure 3.1

SO... YOU WANNA BE A STAR?

We are now casting two major parts for our new short film. Our budget is tight, but we are consummate pros and committed to nothing less than a great movie.

Genre: Drama/Thriller

Synopsis: An ambitious college student tries to cheat his way into Harvard Law School and loses everything in the process.

Schedule of the Shoot: Weekends of July (total of 8 shooting days)

General Requirements:
- Fluent in English and French
- Acting experience preferred
- Should live near Santa Monica

CHARACTERS:

TOMMY
- Lead
- In his early 20's
- Role: college student determined to get into Harvard Law in order to please
  his demanding father
- Tall, handsome, all-American

STEVE
- Lead
- Early 20's
- Role: Tommy's best friend, also intent on Harvard Law; more ruthless than
  Tommy, very persuasive
- Dark good looks, great physical shape

This is a non-union shoot.
We will be paying talent $25/day and providing 3 meals/day plus snacks. Actors will also be given a DVD copy of the finished film.

Please send your resume and photos (one head shot, one full body) to Heidi at
XYZ@XYZ.com

Thank you!

Auditions

THE AUDITION IS A multi-step process. It involves a basic interview to get a sense of the person and an actual reading of key scenes from the script. This first phase (which you should videotape for later review) leads to callbacks. During callbacks you should work more intensively with the auditioning actors, giving them more challenging scenes to read and testing their interaction with other performers. During all these steps, it's very important that you create a relaxed atmosphere.

The interview part of the audition is where you learn what kind of people the actors are and how right they are for a specific role. Even if you feel an actor doesn't physically fit a role, I urge you not to dismiss him/her. At this stage, it's important to keep an open mind, as you may find that an actor's inner life is perfect for the role and so exciting that it trumps any physical traits.

From the moment actors walk in the room, try to put them at ease because if they're nervous, you'll never learn what they're really like and whether you can work effectively with them. I typically break the ice in interviews by asking the actors a couple of social questions, like what drew them to acting in the first place, where they're from, and what they like to do in their spare time. Afterwards, I like to talk about the actor's specific experience and what roles he found most rewarding. Finally, I ask the actor about his impression of the script and characters, specifically how he feels his role fits into the story.

The point of all this is to bring out the actors' personalities—energy, confidence, outlook on life, intelligence—before they read from the script.

During the actor's first reading there are many things to watch for. In fact, there are so many things that you might find yourself blending them into one general goal: to find the perfect actors. Don't do this. Take a deep breath and make sure you don't let yourself get seduced by a good reading and a feeling of overall "rightness." You may learn down the line that the actor was hiding a certain stubbornness regarding the role, or an inability to work well with other actors. Instead, judge the first reading with the following questions in mind:

▶ **Is the actor connected to the role? Does he understand the character and his inner life, or is he just playing the surface and what is obvious?**

▶ **Is he bringing something different to the role?**

▶ **Does he listen well to the person playing opposite and respond in the moment?**

▶ **Do you believe what he's doing?**

Once the actors have read the scene, you should give them a suggestion or two to see how well they respond to direction. For example, you might ask them to change the circumstances of the scene a little bit (or completely), or maybe try a new objective (e.g., instead of trying to seduce the girl, try to repulse her). Don't worry about giving them a change up. Genuine actors love these kinds of challenges.

As I mentioned earlier, it's a good idea to tape your auditions. Not only is it a good way to refresh your memory after you've seen many actors, but it shows you how actors come across onscreen and how they work with other performers. Since you already have a camera (and a tripod, I hope) it won't cost you anything.

Callbacks

After the first audition, you'll produce a short list of actors you want to call back. Callbacks give you the opportunity to "go deeper" with actors and decide who is best for each role. Callbacks also give you a good sense of what kind of directorial approach works best for each actor. Chances are each actor will require a different approach. Some are very thoughtful and like to develop ideas on their own, whereas others require a great deal more input from their director and need to be spoon-fed.

In addition, callbacks allow you to test actors with different partners and assess their responses. One of the most important things about film acting is the ability to be "present," to *listen* and respond to other actors as though their dialogue is being spoken for the first time (even if it's the hundredth time). You'll also find that callbacks reveal chemistry between actors—how responsive they are to each other, how free, sexual tension, and the extent to which this creates onscreen interest and excitement.

One of the things I like to do during callbacks is ask the actors to improvise a scene, to drop the script and "wing it." This is one of the best ways to see how strong an actor's imagination is and how spontaneous he can be. That said, be careful not to get seduced by an actor who is brilliant at improv, as you may find when it comes time to perform the script, he can't deliver the same kind of freshness.

Minors

CASTING ANYONE BELOW THE age of 18 in your movie should be done with extreme caution. Even if you're not paying your actors, you'll probably have to deal with a bunch of child labor laws. These vary from state to state, but I guarantee they will all severely limit the amount of time a kid can work on your film. They will also require that a guardian be present at all times and mandate a laundry list of other things.

Of course, if you're shooting in your backyard and your kid brother is the minor in question, you'll probably get away with sneaking under the radar, but otherwise you're taking a big risk if you choose to duck the authorities. Another solution is to find a legal adult who looks like a teenager and can play young. If you do decide to cast a minor, be sure the kid's parents approve everything in your script well before you start shooting. The last thing in the world you want is Mom and Dad showing up on set and pulling their kid because they disapprove of a scene or story element.

For more information on labor laws for child and teen actors visit:

- ▶ **The Screen Actors Guild (http://www.sag.org/)**
- ▶ **Actors' Equity Association (http://www.actorsequity.org/)**
- ▶ **American Federation of Television & Radio Artists (http://www.aftra.org/aftra/aftra.htm)**
- ▶ **A Minor Consideration (http://www.minorcon.org/)**
- ▶ **BizParentz Foundation (http://www.bizparentz.org/)**
- ▶ **U.S. Department of Labor (http://www.dol.gov/esa/programs/whd/state/childentertain.htm)**

Extras

WHEN IT COMES TO EXTRAS or "background talent," family and close friends are your best bet, as they will stomach the tedium and long waits of a film shoot because they want to support you. If they're not available, you will need to place ads for extras. One of the best sites to place ads for extras is Craigslist.

As with your main actors, it's imperative that you treat your extras well, especially if you need them for more than one day. In addition to paying them a small day rate, I strongly suggest that you offer free meals and screen credit. Also, be sure to have many backup extras in place, as people working for a pittance (or for free) often bail out at the last minute.

The days you're shooting scenes with extras tend to be a bit crazy, as there are more people around than other days and the extras need to be managed. I suggest having a production assistant on set to help direct the extras, especially if they number 10 persons or more. Finally, make sure you have an area for your extras to wait quietly until they are needed.

Animals

EVEN THE MOST TRAINED stage animals in the world are difficult to work with and require enormous patience and time. These animals, which cost a fortune to hire, are almost always accompanied by their trainers on set and *still* it's often a crapshoot as to whether they will perform as you want them to.

On my last movie, we used a stage dog and its professional trainer for a few weeks of shooting and, almost always, it was next to impossible to get the dog to perform even the simplest tasks, such as hopping on to a couch and lying down on a specific mark, or barking on cue (see Figure 3.2). We lost many valuable hours working with the dog and, in the end, I was forced to write him out of several scenes so that we could get back on schedule. And remember, we were using a professional stage animal and its trainer! Imagine now, trying to use your family pet or the like. I strongly recommend that you steer clear of using animals in your movie, at least until you've mastered all other aspects of filmmaking —and have a lot of time and cash to spare!

Figure 3.2
Stage dog, Jellybean. A sweet animal but a pain in the butt to work with. I ultimately had to write him out of several scenes so we could get back on schedule.

Summary

▶ Prepare brief descriptions of all your main characters so you can advertise them.

▶ List your production in acting trade papers, local newspapers, magazines, online, and wherever actors hang out.

▶ Pound the pavement and ask around for recommendations.

▶ Create a relaxed atmosphere for first auditions. Break the ice by asking the actors some social questions.

▶ Give actors a suggestion or two after their first readings to see how they respond to direction.

▶ Be sure to videotape all auditions.

▶ For callbacks, ask actors to improvise a scene to gauge their imaginations and spontaneity.

▶ Be very cautious when casting minors in your movie. Do your homework on child labor laws.

▶ Try to use family and friends as extras. Treat them well.

▶ Animals are difficult to work with and eat up valuable time. Avoid using them.

4

On Acting

THE MOST VALUABLE KNOWLEDGE any director can obtain aside from basic filmmaking is of acting. You can and should read about it, as acting is a legitimate craft covered in countless books. You should also take acting classes wherever they're available in your area, so that you can actually do it and learn what it takes to create a character. This knowledge will help you develop strong working relationships with your actors, as they will see that you fully understand and respect their jobs.

The Actor's Life

AS YOU PROBABLY KNOW, many people go into acting because they want to be "stars." For whatever reason, they have a desperate need to be loved and accepted, and they think acting is the answer, completely disregarding the talent and hard work that goes with the job. Fortunately, these people don't stay in the business long (and for God's sake never hire them!). Genuine actors may crave attention and validation, but their main love is the process of creating a character and expressing themselves in different ways.

The problem with acting as a profession is that it has no security. Jobs are very few and far between. As a result, actors have to constantly prove themselves and face regular rejection, which over time makes them insecure and sensitive to criticism. A good director is always conscious of this reality and gives his actors feedback in a very thoughtful and considerate manner. For example, if an actor isn't giving you what you want, try to shift the blame away from her and direct it at yourself, acknowledging that you made a wrong choice or tried to explore something that lead to a dead end. This way, you preserve your actor's self-confidence, which is crucial to a great performance.

Given the constant stress that actors face, you're likely going to run into some "prickly" ones over the course of your career. Some are profoundly insecure and needy, while others are arrogant and challenge the director and his ideas at every step. Just remember that there's a root to all this: the actor's life. As a director, you must look beyond surface behavior so that you can make a sound judgment about an actor's talent and suitability for your movie.

Types of Actors

THE TOUGH ACTOR. This guy (or gal) is often difficult or moody. In my experience, there are two reasons why an actor displays such behavior. The first has to with his current station in the entertainment business. If he's not a "star" (and let's face it, you won't be directing stars at this level), his life as an actor is one of fierce competition and constant rejection. When he does actually land a part, he's usually treated as a "gun for hire" and rarely involved in any creative decision making. In fact, he's probably worked with many directors who didn't give him any say in character development.

His work is very tough, mentally, emotionally and physically, but he is expected to perform whenever he hears, "Action!," oftentimes over and over again. The end result is he feels like a pawn in a high-stakes game totally out of his control—which makes him testy. You can avoid this problem by involving him in the creative process (which is what a good director does anyway). Treat him like a creative partner, with honesty and courtesy. Don't fawn over him, but be open to his thoughts and communicate with him clearly and constructively. His bad behavior may not disappear overnight, but I promise you it will gradually soften.

The second thing that makes an actor difficult is lack of trust and respect for his director. The single biggest mistake you can make as a director is to not know what you want from your actors. Believe it or not, actors will tolerate (and sometimes admire) all kinds of bullying behavior from their director if they believe he is brilliant, confident, and knows exactly what he's doing. On the other hand, if you show up on set or in rehearsals with a flimsy game plan, trusting you can wing it with everybody's input, you're dead—and so is your movie. Your actors will think you're a hack and question everything you say. They may even try to take over. Always remember: actors need a leader to guide them, someone who knows exactly what he wants. I'm not saying to be close-minded and ignore creative input from your performers, but you should always go in with clear, solid plans. If you decide to change them after a discussion with your actors, so be it. No one will ever accuse you of being indecisive.

THE CHARISMATIC ACTOR. When people say actors have "star quality," they mean that the actors have an innate magnetism that draws people in. We like to watch them. They almost seem to shine. Think of your favorite movie stars; they all have this quality. That's why we pay to see them. As the director of a micro-budget film, you won't be working with Hollywood movie stars, but you will surely come across some actors with star quality during the casting process (see Figure 4.1). When you do, it's important to ask yourself, does this person's strong, distinctive presence fit the role I'm casting or does it over-shadow it? In other words, does the role require star quality or a brave, trained actor who is both willing and able to go beyond his surface charisma and completely immerse himself in the character, to disappear and *become* the character? Asking yourself these questions will serve you well and help you avoid miscasting your movie.

THE SELFISH ACTOR. Since actors are required to create intense feelings, some hold on to their real-life emotions and wallow in them for the sake of their performances. As you can imagine, working with someone who's an emotional wreck isn't much fun. Further, these types of actors often have very little control over their craft, and their performances are usually out of sync with the rest of movie. What's worse, they sometimes ignore their fellow actors, as they are so focused on their own feelings. As a director, it's important that you recognize self-indulgent actors early in the process, so that you can bring them into line, or dismiss them entirely.

Figure 4.1
Dave Watson on the set of my first feature, *River Rats*. A charismatic actor through and through. "The camera loves him," we would often say.

THE IMPULSIVE ACTOR. This type of actor likes to go with his gut. He completely trusts his instincts and follows them with total confidence. The upside of this is that such actors often deliver surprising and exciting performances. The downside is some of his instincts don't fit your film, and you may find yourself wasting a lot of time shooting many takes in order to get what you want. Your job with this type of actor is to provide some story and character bound-aries, while still allowing enough freedom for experimentation.

THE THINKING ACTOR. Though this type of actor is by no means perfect, he is hands down my favorite because he works in a logical manner and does his homework, carefully studying and building his character layer by layer. He also usually possesses a sharp mind and provides many useful ideas. The only drawback to this type is the tendency to rigidly follow guidelines and play it safe. This can result in a predictable performance. If you sense your actor heading down this path, let him know that he's in a safe environment for taking risks and encourage him to let go and try something daring.

THE INSECURE ACTOR. Fear is this type of actor's biggest problem. Fear of rejection, ridicule, failure, etc., regardless of how talented he actually is. In fact, some of the most brilliant performers in history were extremely insecure and would second-guess and triple-check everything they did until they were literally on the verge of a nervous breakdown. Since you don't want to dismiss a talented performer, your job with insecure actors is to a) constantly reassure them and b) create a safe, relaxed environment, which allows them to shed their fears before the camera starts rolling.

THE LAZY ACTOR. Though, in theory, you may able to motivate lazy actors into fresh, exciting work, in my opinion, it's just not worth the risk of hiring them. You have 1,001 other challenges on your plate as a low-budget director. The last thing you need is some mail-it-in type devoid of any creative inspiration who you have to constantly push and prod. You're looking for spirited, driven performers who want to shine as much as you do. If you're smart, you'll have an audition process that identifies and weeds out lazy actors.

The Road to Good Acting

FIRST, LET'S DEFINE GOOD ACTING simply as Truth. Believability. Realism. You get the idea. An actor's responsibility is to create a character whom we the audience see and feel as authentic. Your job as the director is to help your actors reach that end goal, which isn't necessarily a truthful delivery of dialogue. Always remember that words are simply that—words. It's what's *behind the words* that creates believability. An actor's body language, tone of voice, eyes.

The way I approach acting is from "the inside out." I believe that an actor has to internalize a character before he can externalize. He has to understand and, ideally, identify with his character's psychology, life experiences, and so forth. This creates emotions and impulses in the actor that become behavior and, in turn, a truthful performance. There are some schools of thought that champion the idea that physical activity, in and of itself, can trigger emotions. For example, if you pound a table-top with your fist long enough and hard enough you'll start to feel anger. This kind of approach can be useful at times (especially when an actor is blocked up) but, in my opinion, should never come before creating an inner life.

If an actor finds he simply can't connect with his character's life experiences and emotions, a good approach is to substitute a personal experience for that of his character's. For example, let's say an actor has to perform a passionate love scene with an actress he hardly knows. One of the things he can do is imagine somebody he truly loves. Fully imagine the experience, using all his senses. Was it sunny that day? What smells were present? Was he in a comfortable, warm bed? How did his lover taste? By completely recreating this personal experience, the actor is able to generate the emotions required by the scene.

Actors' Needs and Fears

To WORK AT THE TOP of your abilities as a director, you must understand actors' needs and fears. Here are some of the most common.

THE NEED TO SUCCEED. Actors, like the rest of us, want to be the best they can be. It's not just because they're in the public light and face potential embarrassment; it's because they care about what they do and consider themselves professionals. They want to be encouraged (and often pushed) to "reach" and go beyond their previous accomplishments. This encouragement comes from you, the director. Treat your actors with respect and help them strive for the best performances of their lives. This ties in with what is probably the biggest actor need there is, which follows.

THE NEED TO BE DIRECTED. I touched on this earlier in the chapter but it stands repeating in greater detail. Actors want a leader who they trust and respect, someone who understands their craft and communicates freely and clearly. If you haven't done your homework on the script, its characters and their motivations, you can't possibly direct effectively. When actors invariably ask you questions about a scene or their characters, you'll pause, hem and haw, and possibly even say, "I don't know, let me think about it." And that's exactly when you'll lose your actors. Then you're in deep trouble. They'll either try to direct themselves or, worse, just phone in their performances and move on to the next gig.

THE FEAR OF DRYING UP. Filmmaking requires shooting multiple takes of a scene in order to get the best possible footage "in the can." Directors also usually shoot a scene from different angles in order to get coverage, which gives them options in the editing room to pace a scene, shape a performance, etc. All this repetition can be very tough on actors because it can cause them to lose their spark after several takes. They dry up. This can also happen during camera rehearsals when actors are required to run through their actions and dialogue to nail down various technical demands such as lighting, sound, etc. When working with relative newcomers, you should remind them to save their performances for shooting and just go through rehearsals at half-speed. As for "sparking up" an actor's performance after many takes, there are several things you can do to help, which I'll cover in detail in Chapter 5.

THE NEED FOR A SUPPORTIVE SET. A film set with a negative atmosphere can have a very destructive effect on an actor's performance. As the director, you are responsible for the energy and morale on your set. If people are frustrated, hungry, rushed, whatever, it's your fault and you have to fix things immediately. I urge you not to underestimate the importance of creating and nurturing a positive atmosphere on set.

THE NEED TO REHEARSE. Some very successful Hollywood directors do not rehearse their actors until the very day of shooting—and, then, it's only a quick camera rehearsal before actually rolling. These filmmakers argue that rehearsals drain the freshness and excitement out of performances. I am not one of those filmmakers. Rehearsals are invaluable—especially to a low-budget filmmaker who cannot afford to waste time on set discussing things like character motivation and experimenting with various actions, blocking, etc. Rehearsals save you time and money. More important, they allow you to build trusting relationships with your actors. You get to know them socially, you learn how they work, what they need, and they learn the same things about you. Finally, you and your cast can patiently and thoroughly delve into characters and story without the pressures of the set.

THE NEED FOR CREATIVE FREEDOM. Here, you have to walk a fine line. As a director, you don't want to stifle your actors' creativity, but, at the same time, it's imperative that you give them guidance and boundaries. The best way to strike a balance is to come to an agreement with your actors (during rehearsals!) about the purpose and spirit of a scene. Then, within those parameters, give your actors the freedom to create and improvise. One of the most important things you can do as a director is encourage and welcome "happy accidents." Unexpected events and imperfections can improve a scene, sometimes radically. For example, an actor forgetting his lines but continuing with the emotional truth he has generated and delivering some of the best dialogue you've ever heard. Or a slip up in physical action leading to a wonderful moment that no one could have predicted or planned. If you capture just a handful of these moments on film, consider yourself blessed.

Summary

▶ Acting is the most important craft you can learn as a director.

▶ Always be conscious of the challenges and difficulties of an actor's life.

▶ Train yourself to recognize the different types of actors, so that you can deal with them effectively.

▶ Good acting is about Truth. Focus on getting truthful performances, not perfect line readings.

▶ Encourage your actors to internalize their characters before externalizing them.

▶ Educate yourself on common actor needs and fears.

Rehearsing
Your Actors

AS I MENTIONED IN CHAPTER 4, many directors (surprisingly, some very successful ones) choose not to rehearse their actors before shooting begins. This is actually quite common in the film and TV business. Many directors are so focused on the technology of filmmaking that they don't give rehearsals a second thought, ignoring the human component of their own movies. Others point to the nature of filmmaking itself as an argument against rehearsing. They contend that you can shoot many takes of a performance and edit them together later for the best possible result. Others still argue that rehearsals can sap a performance of its freshness and excitement.

There is some truth to these arguments, as I have seen horrible performances literally transformed into great ones in the editing room. And I have seen certain scenes rehearsed to death until the actors were literally behaving like zombies. However, I would never in a million years fully depend on technology, editing tricks, or luck to generate strong performances in my films. Rehearsals are crucial. They allow a director to focus on his actors without the distractions and pressures of a set. They allow the entire company to exchange ideas in a relaxed atmosphere, and allow director and actor to thoughtfully, carefully develop a character. There is also an invaluable social component to rehearsals: people get to know each other and bond. Finally, the director is given an opportunity to share in detail his vision for the film with his cast.

The First Read-Through

THE FIRST READ-THROUGH is when the director and his entire cast sit down together (usually for the first time), read the script out loud, and discuss it afterwards (see Figure 5.1). This is where you'll find out how each actor interprets the story and how well the characters are fitting together. You'll probably also start to see where your biggest problems are, both in terms of script and actors.

I like to read through the script in one go, instead of reading it in sections. That way, everyone gets a sense of the piece as a whole. After the reading, I always have a set of questions ready for the actors, to spark discussion. Despite having strong ideas myself, I want to hear their thoughts (and criticisms) about the story, the themes, the characters, and so forth. I treat them as creative partners and encourage them to roll up their sleeves and dig in. Given the energy a group brings to any project, this process often uncovers aspects of the script that never occurred to you. As a result, your film improves and deepens. Certainly, any actor worth his salt loves this approach because it respects his intelligence and gives him an opportunity to contribute. As a director, this approach is also important because it discourages your cast from depending on you for small details.

During the read-through I strongly suggest that you take notes so that you don't lose any important ideas or impressions that may come to mind. I guarantee you'll be thankful you did, as by this point in the process, you're going to be dealing with a 1,001 things all at once and your memory is going to fail you every now and then. With notes (or better yet, an audio recording) you won't overlook or forget anything. Most important, your actors will see that you're focused and prepared.

At this stage, make it absolutely clear that you don't want anyone to learn lines yet. Memorizing lines tends to lock an actor into a certain interpretation of his character. Since you and your cast are still exploring the story and characters (and possibly making changes), it's important to wait. Finally, before your actors leave for the day give them a rehearsal schedule and give them a homework assignment: to develop biographies for their characters—backstories, important life experiences, attitudes, value systems, etc.

Figure 5.1

Creating a Relaxed Atmosphere

FOR ACTORS TO BE THE BEST they can be, they need to free their imaginations. They need to be excited about what they're doing, anxious to create, and confident they can go anywhere and try anything. It's your job as the director to make all this possible. But without relaxation, it's not going to happen.

Tension is an actor's worst enemy. It doesn't matter what its source—a foolish director, annoying castmates, problems at home—they all result in the same thing, block up. Tension prevents actors from concentrating and releasing their emotions in a truthful way. In other words, it cripples them and makes them look bad.

As I stressed earlier, a director puts his actors at ease by respecting them and including them in the creative process. If you can create an atmosphere that says, "We're a team," you will have gone a long way toward reducing your actors' tensions. Also, at the beginning of each day's work, interact with the actors, shoot the breeze while trying to measure how they're feeling. Are they stressed or energized? Depressed or physically exhausted? By figuring out their moods, you'll get an idea what they need from you that day—e.g., more support, patience, etc.

Another way to create a strong team dynamic is to socialize a little bit with your actors outside the confines of your rehearsal space. On all my films, I've made an effort to go out for drinks, meals, etc. with my actors after rehearsals. I've even invited them to movies that I was excited to see, so that we could discuss them afterwards and exchange creative ideas. This kind of socializing goes a long way toward relaxing your actors and getting them to bond with you and each other.

The Director-Actor Relationship

IT MAY SOUND PAINFULLY obvious, but the most important thing between a director and actor is communication (see Figure 5.2). If a director can't clearly communicate to his actors how well they're creating their characters and scenes, then he's in deep trouble. If you see something that needs work, it's crucial that you express yourself in a way that leads your actors to what you want. Again, it may sound like simple advice, but you would be amazed at how many directors aren't clear about what they want or totally lack the necessary language skills to communicate effectively. If the actors in such a case are also poor communicators, then there's very little hope of making a good movie.

To develop strong communication skills, the director must first look at his attitude. Is he a collaborator or a bully? The former leads to relaxed actors, and the latter leads to tense ones. That's not to say a director needs agreement from his actors on all things, but simply that he must respect their opinions and involve them in his process.

Secondly, a director must be a confident leader and know exactly where he wants his film to go. This kind of leadership comes from extreme preparation *before* rehearsals. Don't be lazy. Cover everything. Know your story through and through, including its subplots, themes and, of course, characters—their backgrounds, values, life views, their very souls. Further, have strong opinions on all these aspects. How do *you* see things? Only with intelligent answers will you gain respect and trust from your actors and be able to have productive communications with them.

One word of caution: unless it's early in rehearsals and you and your cast are delving deeply into the story and characters, try to be specific and concise with your directions. Long-winded explanations of story and themes tend to confuse and numb actors, and rarely lead to strong results. When it comes to actually rehearsing a scene, the more exact and brief you are, the better. And that doesn't mean bluntly telling an actor what result you want (e.g., "Hug her when she comes through the door.")

This kind of direction leads to playing a mechanical behavior, to surface acting. It's not rooted in character or emotional truth. Instead, try to deal with a character's objective or goal: what he or she is trying to achieve in the scene. For example, instead of giving a results-based direction like, "Hug her," you might suggest, "Make her feel loved."

Figure 5.2
Cathy Reddy and I discussing the script on the set of *River Rats* (1995).

Common Acting Problems and Solutions

LACK OF PRESENCE. Here, I don't mean a lack of stage presence or star quality, I mean a lack of emotional presence. When an actor is not responding to his environment and what others in the scene are doing, he is not present—i.e., he is not listening with all his senses and *reacting* spontaneously. He is acting by himself, with no real connection to his partners. In order to encourage the give-and-take process that is crucial to good acting, a director should make sure that an actor always has a strong goal that connects him to the scene and other actors. Even if an actor has no dialogue and is simply listening to a couple argue, for example, he should still have a strong objective to play. Perhaps he's internally rooting for the woman, or maybe he's aching to stop the fight before it gets out of hand but can't muster the nerve.

PUSHING. This happens when an actor feels a trace of real emotion inside himself and "pushes" it into existence, instead of trusting it to grow naturally and truthfully. In other words, he over-does it, afraid that what he's feeling won't reach the audience otherwise. You see this a lot when an actor is trying to show extreme anger. He feels a germ of real anger then pushes it into a scream of rage, distorting his face and tightening his muscles. It looks fake because the actor is expressing what he *thinks* is right, not what he *feels* is right. He's watching himself and cut off from his character. In reality, we usually tighten our muscles to control our anger, not release it.

The main cause of pushing is tension, both physical and emotional. Your job is to help your actors relax so they can reconnect with their characters and feelings. When dealing with physical tension, simple breathing exercises will often do the trick: taking a series of long, deep breaths and exhaling completely. Another effective method is to systematically relax one part of the body at a time. For example, start with the eyes, then move to the jaw, and slowly down the rest of the body. Surprisingly, sometimes a completely different approach works: making your actors run and jump around until their hearts are racing. This often has an energizing effect and allows actors to shake off any tension, worries, distractions.

INDICATING. This means that an actor is using external, physical ways to show what his character is feeling. In other words, the actor is using predictable (sometimes cliched) surface behavior to show an emotion. For example, gritting his teeth to show anger, or scratching his head to show concentration. An actor who indicates is not creating emotion from within. He has not connected to his character on a deep personal level. Sometimes the actor is just tired, unprepared, or lazy, which you can address as you see fit. Other times, the actor will need your help to personally identify with his character and the circumstances of the scene. Talk him through it, making sure that he verbalizes step by step what his character is experiencing throughout the scene. This method often helps an actor focus and get back on track.

NUMBNESS. Sometimes an actor will seem to lose his or her spark, and the scene will just die. This can be the result of repetition (which is part of filmmaking and unavoidable), tiredness, loss of focus, etc. If your actor is using substitution (covered in Chapter 4), it's possible that the personal experience he's been recalling to create emotions has dried up. In such a case, one way to help him get back on track is to suggest that he focus on different details of the same experience, to spice it up, in a sense. Alternatively, you might suggest that he focus on a new personal experience that evokes the same feelings. Another effective approach is to have the actor "raise the stakes" of the scene. In other words, have him imagine more dire consequences of not achieving his character goal in the scene.

Improvisation

MOST PEOPLE HAVE HEARD about improvisation and believe it's basically creating a performance on the spot, with no preparation or idea of what's coming next and just following your instincts. Though there is some truth to this, improvisation is actually much more complex. Further, many people believe that movies are often made through improv, due largely to the press around famous directors who work with actors in this fashion. The truth is, improv can be a valuable tool both in rehearsals and during production but can also be a trap that wastes valuable time and money. The trick is in fully understanding improv and knowing how to use it to your movie's advantage.

Since actors obviously know ahead of time how the movie unfolds and what their lines and actions are, it can sap their drive and the freshness of their performances. Improv forces an actor to truly look and listen to his partners and react in the moment, with no script or knowledge of what's coming next. It can therefore free an actor of staleness and mechanical behavior and help him connect more deeply with his character. But before trying improv, an actor must clearly understand his character's needs and objectives in the scene —what lies *beneath* the script's text. Only then, when he personally relates to his character, can he try something spontaneous.

If the improv is a success and your scene comes alive, it's crucial that you zero in on what *specifically* made it successful. Did the actor discover something inside himself during the improv (perhaps a personal parallel) that made the scene fly? If so, he must be conscious of it and use it when returning to the script. If the improv fails and seems dead, it's probably because the actor is trying to rewrite the scripted dialogue in his head instead of connecting to his character and the circumstances of the scene. As the director, you must watch for this.

Another way you can use improv to punch up a scene is to completely take away your actors' dialogue. I know it sounds crazy but by playing the scene without words your actors will be forced to interact with their eyes and body language. They will be free of their scripted lines and naturally connect with their characters' needs/objectives and the reality of the scene. When you return to the script, I'm sure you'll find a big improvement.

Strengthening Character Relationships

A S I MENTIONED EARLIER, one of the great things about rehearsals is the opportunity for actors to get to know each other on a personal level. This is particularly helpful if the relationships that develop between actors strengthen the relationships between characters. For example, if your leading man and lady fall for each other in real life, and the characters they're playing are also in love, you've caught a break (see Figure 5.3). Their real affections will translate to the screen and their performances will feel truthful.

As a director, you should always keep an eye out for actor relationships that can improve your movie and do whatever you can to encourage them. Take, for example, two characters who are supposed to hate each other. If you notice that there's already a bit of friction between the two actors playing these parts, you might consider nurturing that friction—perhaps keep them apart before they can get more comfortable with each other. Or, if you're feeling brave, actually do something that turns their friction into genuine animosity. Be very careful, however, when playing this kind of twisted matchmaker, for it can backfire and create such hostility that your actors block up and are unable to concentrate. Walk a very fine line.

Figure 5.3
Mark and Heather Woods who met on my first short film many years ago. From the beginning, there was a strong attraction between them, which I encouraged, as they were playing a young couple in love. Mark and Heather eventually married.

The Value of Using Your Sets

USING YOUR SETS DURING rehearsals is considered a luxury in the movie business. Most of the time, sets have not been fully constructed or dressed while rehearsals are taking place, and the director and actors have to imagine locations and their geography. I had to face this challenge on my last movie, *Alone With Her*. Due to various scheduling problems, our sets were under construction until the very day before we started shooting. We therefore had to rehearse among tools, scaffolding, and dry wall, and struggle to "get in the zone." As you can see in Figures 5.4 to 5.7, it would have been easier and much more effective to rehearse on the finished sets.

Figure 5.4
Kitchen set under construction.

Figure 5.5
Kitchen set complete.

Figure 5.6
Living room and bedroom sets under construction.

Figure 5.7
Finished bedroom set.

Since you're shooting a micro-budget film and are likely using real, existing locations that are "ready to go," you should do everything in your power to rehearse on set. It will enrich your actors' performances and your scenes.

Take, for example, a scene that takes place in a busy bar. A man and woman have met for the first time and are becoming attracted to each other. How each of them physically relates to the bar will tell us a great deal about how they feel. Is the woman gently picking at her straw, suggesting sexual tension? Is the man using the loud music as an excuse to lean closer to the woman so that he can hear what she's saying? Are they completely focused on each other despite the distracting crowd? Location details like these can provide wonderful acting opportunities and greatly improve your movie. Always search for them and, when necessary, create them.

Summary

▶ Rehearsals are crucial to the success of your movie. The more time you can devote to them, the better.

▶ Have some questions ready after the first read-through to engage your actors in creative discussions. Be sure to take notes, and insist that your actors not commit to their lines yet.

▶ Create a relaxed atmosphere for rehearsals, so your actors feel comfortable to try anything and go anywhere.

▶ For the best possible relationships with your actors, be extremely prepared. Have strong, clear ideas about the script, its themes and characters. Only with intelligent answers will you gain the respect and trust of your actors.

▶ Try to be concise with your directions and base them on character objectives and goals.

▶ Familiarize yourself with common acting problems and solutions.

▶ Improvisation can be very useful in livening up a stale scene, but before trying it an actor must be aware of his character's needs and objectives in the scene. He must know what's *beneath* the script's words.

▶ Encourage relationships between actors that strengthen relationships between characters.

▶ Use your sets during rehearsals, as it will enrich your actors' performances.

The Shooting Script

and Storyboards

AS THE DIRECTOR OF A NO-BUDGET movie, you *must* have a clear, detailed plan of attack when it comes to shooting. You just can't afford to cover every scene from 10 different camera angles then sort through all the footage in the editing room for months (if not years) on end. Further, without a specific game plan, your cast and crew will see that you don't really know what you want, and they'll quickly lose faith in your abilities and leadership.

You must therefore know *before* shooting how each of your scenes is going to cut together and film only what you need for the editing room. That's where the shooting script comes in. It's your playbook for turning your screenplay into a movie. In addition to your shooting script, you may want to create some corresponding diagrams, also known as *storyboards*, which will visualize how you plan to shoot particularly challenging sequences, such as action scenes or complicated camera moves.

From Screenplay to Shooting Script

THE SHOOTING SCRIPT IS usually one of the last things you prepare, after considerable rehearsals, location scouting, and long talks with your director of photography—which, in this case, may be you—about what camera and lighting equipment you need and can afford. From your rehearsals, you have probably gotten a strong sense of how you want to shoot your scenes. If you're still not 100% there, take a few days (or longer) to sit down in a quiet, private room and visualize each scene. Be sure to keep in mind that a scene's design should be based on its purpose in the story; in other words, what the audience needs to know about the setting, characters, their relationships, and so forth (see Chapter 8 for the basics of effectively staging scenes).

Once you've put your plans to paper, discuss them with your director of photography, as he or she will no doubt have valuable input. The next step is to expand your screenplay, which so far doesn't contain any camera directions. With a simple pencil, number your scenes and specify your camera directions, as shown in Figure 6.1. Note that there is an overlap from shot to shot. This is necessary for editing (covered in Chapter 10).

Finally, keep in mind that your shooting script will likely change as you create your schedule, lock down locations, and hire cast and crew. Your mind will be constantly working on the movie, revising scenes, coming up with new ideas, strategies, etc. Be flexible. Your shooting script is not written in stone; it's organic, constantly growing, changing, improving—like your entire movie.

Figure 6.1

49

Tommy's POV thru windshield and looking at Sandra

INT. TOMMY'S HONDA (MOVING) - DAY

Tommy drives through a wealthy New England neighborhood, gazing through the windshield with homesick eyes: familiar houses, faces passing by, snow-covered pines, Christmas lights. Sandra riding in the passenger's seat, holding Tommy's hand, a holiday glow about her.

Sandra's POV of Tommy

Master Shot

EXT. GREENE FAMILY HOME - DAY

A sleek, modern house exuding warmth and security. Tommy's Honda pulls into the driveway alongside a BMW and a station wagon. The moment he and Sandra reach the front steps, Tommy's mom rushes out the door in her slippers, beaming.

Handheld Medium Shots

                    MOM
          Well look what the cat dragged in...!

She wraps her loving arms around Tommy and hugs him tight as Tommy's kid SISTER appears at the doorway in adorable Christmas pyjamas, delighted to see her big brother.

                    TOMMY
          Mom, it's cold. C'mon...

They head indoors, exchanging pleasantries, Tommy picking up his sister and nuzzling her neck as she squeals with glee.

INT. FOYER - TOMMY'S HOUSE

MS

                    TOMMY'S MOM (feeling his coat)
          When are you going to buy a warmer
          jacket?

                    TOMMY'S FATHER
            (appearing from the living room)
          Enough already, he's been here thirty
          seconds...How are you, Sandra?

Medium Shot

                    SANDRA
          Merry Christmas, Mr. Greene.

2 Shot

They exchange pecks on the cheek and Dad turns to Tommy. Warmly shakes his hand, eyes filled with pride.

                    FATHER
          How'd exams go?

                    TOMMY
          Pretty good.

Over the shoulder - both

Types of Shots

THE FOLLOWING LIST BRIEFLY describes the most common types of shots. Keep in mind that the exact terminology may vary from production to production, but the basic principles are the same. I start by listing the types of static shots, then move on to different kinds of camera movements.

EWS (Extreme Wide Shot)

This type of shot is often referred to as an "establishing shot," meaning that it's designed to show the audience where the scene is taking place and what the surroundings are (see Figures 6.2 and 6.3). It is therefore often the first shot in a scene. The EWS is also known as an Extreme Long Shot.

In addition to Figures 6.2 and 6.3, I have provided a cinematic example from my first feature film, *River Rats*, which can be viewed on the DVD included with this book.

Figure 6.2

Figure 6.3

Wide Shot (WS)

In this shot, your subject takes up the full frame. If it's a character, he's usually shown from head to toe, as in Figure 6.4. If it's a location, a large part of it is shown. See the DVD for more examples.

Figure 6.4

Medium Shot (MS)

This shot shows your subject in more detail. When shooting a person, it usually means from the waist up (see Figure 6.5 and the DVD for examples). This is basically how you would see a person in real life if you were having a conversation. It's a safe, casual shot that allows some space for movement and hand gestures. Obviously, if you're looking to capture emotion a closer shot would be more effective.

Figure 6.5

Close-Up (CU)

In a close-up, a certain part of your subject takes up the whole frame. When shooting a person, it usually means a close-up of the face (see Figure 6.6 and the DVD for examples). This shot is most effective when you're looking to capture emotion as you are drawn in to the character's personal space and can clearly see his eyes and facial expressions.

Figure 6.6

Extreme Close-Up (ECU)

As the name suggests, this shot brings you very close to the subject and shows extreme detail (see Figure 6.7 and the DVD for examples).

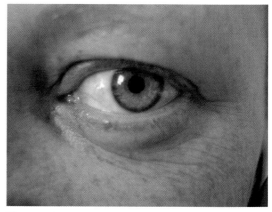

Figure 6.7

Two Shot (TS)

A two shot puts two people in view, often from the waist up (see Figure 6.8 and the DVD for examples). It establishes the relationship between two subjects and allows them to interact with some movement within the frame. Obviously, this shot can be split up into two separate one shots. A three shot, of course, would frame three subjects, and a group shot would show four characters or more.

Figure 6.8

Over-the-Shoulder Shot (OSS)

This is one of the most popular shots in cinema. As the name suggests, it's a view of the subject from behind someone, over his or her shoulder (see Figure 6.9 and the DVD for examples). It's usually used in two-way conversations and shows the position of each person.

Figure 6.9

Low Angle

This is a shot that looks up, usually at a character, and makes him or her seem more powerful (see Figure 6.10).

Figure 6.10

High Angle

This shot looks down, again usually at a person, and makes him or her seem more vulnerable (see Figure 6.11).

Point-of-View Shot (POV)

This shot is also extremely popular and effective. It shows a view from a character's perspective, through his or her eyes. This is a very subjective shot, which tends to makes us strongly identify with the character because we are put in his or her shoes, so to speak.

Figure 6.11

Dutch Angle

This shot is created when the camera is slanted at an angle, making the image off-balance (see Figure 6.12). It is often used to suggest something is wrong, strange, or out of control.

Figure 6.12

Dolly Shot

This moving shot involves mounting your camera on a cart that travels along tracks laid down on the floor or ground. The camera shoots your subject as it moves. Dolly shots can provide dramatic effect but are time-consuming to set up. Use them sparingly, given your low budget. An alternative "poor man's version" uses a wheelchair where someone sits holding the camera while another person pushes.

Crane Shot

This shot is taken by a camera on a crane and is usually used to show characters or action from above. The shot can "crane up" or "crane down" while moving horizontally, if desired. Though most cranes are large, expensive, automated machines that you can't afford, there are some smaller, manual ones called "jibs" that move up and down about 10 feet. Still, they're tough to operate and can eat up valuable time.

Following Shot

As you might guess, this shot follows the subject as it moves. The shot can be performed with a dolly, hand-held camera, or a Steadicam. The Steadicam is a special mechanical harness that holds the camera and virtually eliminates any shaking or unsteadiness. It's operated by a professional cameraman and is probably too expensive for your shoot. See the DVD for examples of hand-held and Steadicam shots.

Panning Shot

A pan is a horizontal camera movement where your camera moves left or right while on a stationary location, usually a tripod (see Figures 6.13, 6.14, and the DVD for examples). This shot is comparatively easier to pull off than a dolly or follow shot, and you will probably be using it a great deal.

Figure 6.13

Figure 6.14

Tilting Shot

This shot is a vertical camera movement where your camera *tilts* up or down, again while fixed on a tripod (see Figures 6.15, 6.16, and the DVD for examples).

Figure 6.15

Figure 6.16

Zooming Shot

This shot isn't really a camera move, but it *looks* like one. It involves changing the focal length of your camera lens (usually by simply pressing a button) to magnify part of the image. Most of us, at one time or another, have used the zoom function on our camcorders. It's an easy shot to perform and perhaps that's why it's considered somewhat amateurish. Use it sparingly (if at all) because it doesn't quite match the dramatic effect of a true moving shot like a dolly or follow. See the DVD for examples.

Coverage

OVERAGE REFERS TO THE number of camera setups (and corresponding angles) you use to film a scene and the amount of footage you shoot. The more coverage you shoot, the more choices and control you have when editing your movie. On the other hand, shooting a lot of coverage requires a lot of time (and money). As I said earlier, given your budget, it's important that you visualize your movie as much as possible (editing every scene in your head) and shoot what you need.

As a precaution, however, I recommend that you try to cover each scene from at least two different angles so you don't find yourself completely handcuffed in the editing room. You may discover, for example, that a scene you imagined as one long continuous shot is playing too slowly and that you want to shorten it. With coverage from a different angle you can edit down the scene by effectively cutting back and forth between two angles. Without the additional coverage, you may find yourself stuck with no way out.

The safest and most traditional way to cover a scene is to shoot a wide angle (or Master Shot) first then move in for closer coverage. By starting with your master, it's easier to ensure lighting continuity (matching) than if you go from close-ups to wider shots. It also makes it easier to protect other aspects of continuity such as action and dialogue, since the master fully covers the scene and establishes for the actors what words and actions to repeat in closer shots. Further, by getting your master first it gives you some comfort in knowing that you have your whole scene on film. If you end up running out of time or some problem comes up and you're not able to get close-ups or additional coverage, you at least have all the lines and actions in your pocket.

An important note on masters: they don't have to be entirely perfect. Since you're shooting your scene from at least one other angle (and hopefully more), you'll have the coverage you need in the editing room, so don't kill valuable time shooting a dozen master shots of a scene. Flubbed lines and actions can be easily edited out with your other footage. For that reason, make sure you instruct your actors to keep going if they slip up during a master shot. The only reason they should stop is if you say, "Cut!"

Storyboards

STORYBOARDS ARE VISUAL representations of shots. They can be professionally rendered full-color artwork, simple black-and-white diagrams, or even stick-figure sketches. In the end, they all accomplish the same thing— they clearly communicate your shooting plans to your cast and crew, and save you oceans of time and money on the set. Many professional film-makers storyboard their entire films, leaving nothing to chance or misunderstanding. At the very least, you should create storyboards for any action scenes or complex camera moves that you're planning for your movie.

Figure 6.17 shows an example of a storyboard. The shot's description is printed directly underneath the storyboard panel. If there's dialogue, it goes under the description.

DESCRIPTION OF SHOT HERE
DIALOGUE HERE

Figure 6.17

Sometimes several storyboards are needed to explain the stages of a moving shot, as shown in Figure 6.18, which illustrates an uninterrupted crane shot of a simple table.

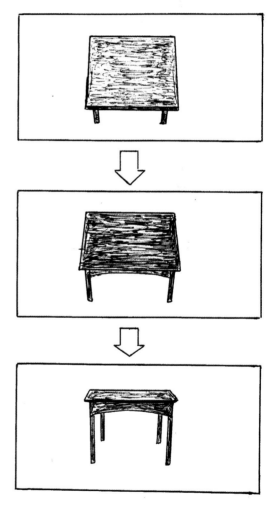

Figure 6.18

Arrows outside the frame indicate camera movement (see Figures 6.19 to 6.23).

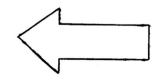

PAN

DOLLY OUT

(OR MOVE OUT W/ HANDHELD CAMERA)

Figure 6.19

Figure 6.22

CRANE

DOLLY IN

(OR MOVE IN W/ HANDHELD CAMERA)

Figure 6.20

Figure 6.23

Arrows inside the frame indicate the movement of a subject, usually your actors (see Figure 6.24).

DOLLY AROUND

Figure 6.21

Figure 6.24

Summary

▶ When directing a low-budget movie, have a detailed game plan in place before shooting. Pre-visualize everything.

▶ Carefully prepare your shooting script and storyboards. Be sure to consult with your director of photography and other key crewmembers, as they will have valuable advice.

▶ Educate yourself on the various types of shots and their dramatic effects.

▶ When shooting, be sure to cover each scene from at least two different angles.

▶ Storyboards are invaluable directing tools, especially when planning complicated shots, action scenes, etc.

How to Compose
Great Shots

THE KEY TO A GREAT SHOT is almost always in its composition. As the director, your job is to compose each shot so that all its parts—subject, lighting, background, etc.—work together to create an image with meaning and maximum impact. Each element is crucial to the whole. In a sense, you're the composer using all the instruments in your orchestra to create a masterpiece.

Learning to See with a Director's Eye

SOME PEOPLE ARE NATURALS when it comes to composition. They have great visual instincts and know how to set up an amazing shot right away. But most of us need to tinker around a bit and experiment before we start seeing balance and beauty in the frame. And that's fine. As an amateur filmmaker, you're in the fortunate position of being able to try different things and not worry about the "time is money" clock that weighs down professional directors every day. So adjust your camera, subject, and other elements to your heart's content until you're confident you have an image that is truly impressive.

An instrument that many directors find helpful for composing shots is the camera's viewfinder. By moving around while looking through the viewfinder, you can focus on important elements and isolate them from the overall view. In other words, you're imposing "the frame" on the world you see. The result is often discovering interesting shots that you may not have noticed before. For example, looking at a simple chair through your viewfinder reveals a number of interesting possibilities. From above, looking straight down at the chair, its shape and outline change to something unusual and the floor becomes the background, thus giving the shot immediate attention (see Figure 7.1).

Figure 7.1

Alternatively, if you stay at floor level and move in very close to the chair, interesting lines, textures, and patterns may emerge, as shown in Figure 7.2.

Figure 7.2

Positioning Your Subject

S THE DIRECTOR, YOU MUST always ask yourself, "What is the subject of my shot, and how do I show it in the most effective way possible?" In other words, what is your shot about? What are you trying to emphasize? A mood? A relationship between two characters? The answer will largely dictate how you position your subject, which in most cases, will be your actor(s).

The most obvious position for your subject is right in the center of the frame, where you can clearly and fully see it. This gives the shot geometric balance that is generally pleasing to the eye and works well for strong, sharply drawn shapes and for characters doing something active, as shown Figure 7.3.

If you're going to compose a shot in this way, be sure to position the most important part of your subject slightly above the geometric center of the shot, as most people instinctively prefer to look at a point in that area.

Another popular way to compose a strong, balanced shot is to use "The Rule of Thirds," which has been around for centuries. This rule imagines your shot divided into horizontal and vertical thirds. The intersecting lines create four ideal points for positioning your subject (see Figures 7.4 and 7.5).

Figure 7.3

Figure 7.4

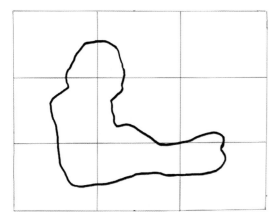

Figure 7.5

The position of the little girl makes her head and torso dominate the composition, which creates a shot with impact. A lower placement of the girl's head and upper body would have included more distracting background, creating a weaker shot. Obviously, you don't want to use this rule all the time, or your style will get repetitive—and boring! Again, always let the dramatic purpose of your shot guide you.

Another option is to occasionally place your subject off center, which is a great way to create emphasis in your shot—to make the audience look straight at your subject. For example, in Figure 7.6, the shot may seem completely unbalanced, with the father and child pushed to the left side of the frame. But they are actually balanced by the landscape and trees, which also connect them personally to this nature scene.

Figure 7.6

Another effect of leaving a lot of empty space around your subject is to emphasize loneliness or isolation, as in Figure 7.7, where the little girl appears totally alone and overshadowed by the landscape.

In the end, as I mentioned earlier, you should always strive to experiment with positioning your subject. Try several options before finalizing the shot. It's your privilege as a novice filmmaker, and you should take full advantage as much as possible.

Figure 7.7

Using Background and Foreground

MANY AMATEUR DIRECTORS concentrate on their subject and give little, if any, serious thought to background and foreground. Yet both of these compositional tools are of crucial importance to getting a great shot. They can provide more important information about your subject, add balance to your shot, and even frame it in a compelling way.

When considering your background, try to watch for these three things:

Figure 7.8

▶ **Extra Limbs.** Be careful there aren't any "extra limbs" like branches or lampposts hidden in your background, which can appear to be growing out of your actor's head (see Figure 7.8). Usually, a simple shift of your camera's position solves the problem, separating your subject from any "limbs."

▶ **Clutter and Confusion.** Another common problem is a busy or jumbled background, which can confuse an otherwise nice shot. Again, simply changing your camera's position can solve this problem. If your background is fixed and can't be avoided, then try to put it out of focus so that your subject stands out, as shown in Figure 7.9

Figure 7.9

▶ **Distracting Light or Color.** For example, a bright light in the upper corner of your frame (or a bright red chair in the background) may draw your attention away from your actor (see Figure 7.10).

Figure 7.10

The foreground is usually neglected even more than the background, which oftentimes is a lost opportunity to really improve your shot. Some effective ways to use foreground:

▶ **To Create Depth.** Imagine a simple shot of a baker kneading some dough, with the baker dead center in the frame, and very little of his surroundings visible. Now imagine that same baker positioned higher in the frame, with a vast array of his breads and pastries in the foreground. Suddenly, the shot says much more about your subject and also gives an impression of depth and scale. The use of foreground in this way "brings the audience" into the shot, as shown in the difference between Figures 7.11 and 7.12.

Figure 7.11

Figure 7.12

▶ **To Frame Your Shot.** The foreground doesn't always have to be at the bottom of your shot. It can also act as a partial or complete frame for your subject. Some examples of foreground frames include windows, doorways, gates, and tree branches (see Figure 7.13). Usually, these frames are most effective when they're in silhouette or out of focus, so that they don't dominate your shot and draw the audience's attention away from your main subject.

Figure 7.13

The Main Outline of Your Shot

I F YOU REDUCE A GREAT SHOT to a simple penciled sketch, to only its shapes and lines, you'll find that it's well balanced and pleasing to the eye. That's because the shot's basic foundation is strong and sound. A good exercise to train yourself in recognizing a strong foundation is to trace the dominant lines and shapes of shots you love and compare them to the outlines of shots you hate. You'll see very quickly which elements contribute to a poor shot and a good one. It's crucial that you notice the lines and shapes of your subject while looking through your viewfinder, before you start shooting. Here are a few things to keep in mind:

▶ **Contrast is an excellent way to make the audience focus on your subject. This can be achieved with both shape and color. For example, a bright red canoe on a blue lake captures the eye much more than a blue canoe would. And the dark shape of a tree standing tall against a gray winter sky makes for a bold contrast (see Figure 7.14).**

Figure 7.14

▶ The mood of a shot can be greatly affected by lines and shape. When strong, diagonal lines dominate a shot, a confident and dynamic quality tends to be created. Whereas the horizontal lines you often find in landscape shots create a more restful and passive mood. Obviously, contrasting these shapes and lines at different angles creates a busy and exciting image, as shown in Figure 7.15.

▶ Changing your camera position can help you manipulate the shapes and lines in your shot. For example, the image of a peaceful river can be given some extra punch by repositioning your camera so that the vigorous, diagonal lines of some tree branches enter the foreground (see Figure 7.16).

Figure 7.16

Figure 7.15

Tone and Contrast

THE THREE-DIMENSIONAL LOOK of a photograph is created by the various tones in the shot and how they differ from each other. Even a cloud, for example, is rarely completely white; it's usually different shades of gray. It is this "tonal contrast" that gives the cloud depth and form.

The best way to affect the tone of your shot is with light. If you place a smooth white ball in front of a white wall and light them from the front so no shadows are created, you won't be able to tell them apart. You'll just have a white blur. But if you move your light to the side to create shadows, the difference will be immediately visible, as shown in Figure 7.17.

Figure 7.17

The ball will develop a full range of tones from white on the lit side to shades of gray to black in the deepest shadows. Your shot will be three-dimensional. You see this kind of contrast in life all the time: the sun's bright light on trees, people, and buildings, which creates solid tones with sharply defined steps (high contrast), or the soft light of a cloudy day, which produces gently changing tones with barely visible edges (low contrast).

Obviously, the tonal contrast of your shot greatly affects its mood. A picture with a lot of dark tones gives a somber and serious impression (see Figure 7.18).

Figure 7.18

However, a shot with a full range of tones, bright highlights, and crisp shadows creates a lively and upbeat atmosphere (see Figure 7.19).

A shot consisting of soft, light tones has a gentle and often romantic quality (see Figure 7.20).

As a director, you should never squander the control you have over your shot's tone. Take the time to carefully consider the effects of light on your subject and the mood you want to create.

Figure 7.19

Figure 7.20

Giving Your Shots Depth

IRST, LET ME STRESS that many great shots lack depth (a three-dimensional quality). Full-frame close-ups of people's faces are often impressive because of their flatness and singular focus, as shown in Figure 7.21.

Figure 7.21

But for many subjects, a flat shot would be a major let down. Landscape shots, for example, only come to life when the audience is pulled into the scenery and is able to look around and explore the image. The same holds true for myriad other images. Therefore, every time you line up a shot, be sure to ask yourself, do I want to create a flat design or a strong, three-dimensional effect? The following elements produce a sense of depth in shots:

▶ **Decreasing Size.** Objects appear to get smaller in a shot as they get farther away, as shown with lampposts in Figure 7.22. Using a wide-angle lens (which keeps your entire shot in focus), you can create a greater feeling of depth.

Figure 7.22

▶ **Engaging Lines.** Lines can create a feeling a depth by drawing the audience into your shot. These lines can come from the top, bottom, or sides of your frame. Compare Figures 7.23 and 7.24 and you'll see what I mean. Figure 7.23 has much less depth than 7.24 because the engaging lines have been cropped out.

Figure 7.23

Figure 7.24

▶ **Overlapping Shapes.** When one shape stands partially in front of another, the sense of depth is greater than if the two shapes are separated. This is illustrated by Figures 7.25 and 7.26.

▶ **Foreground Focus.** This technique is particularly effective for creating strong depth in close-up shots. By putting the background out of focus, you can make your main subject (which is sharply focused) stand out from the rest of the image. The blurry background seems farther away from the main subject than it really is, producing an illusion of depth.

Figure 7.25

Figure 7.26

Summary

▶ Composing a great shot involves taking full advantage of all parts of the image—subject, lighting, background, etc.—and harmonizing them for maximum impact.

▶ Though some people are naturals when it comes to composition, most of us need to experiment with a camera to develop strong instincts.

▶ As the director, always ask yourself, "What is the subject of my shot, and how do I show it in the most effective way possible?"

▶ Educate yourself on the principles of effective composition.

Staging Scenes—
The Basics

I N THIS CHAPTER, I WILL be looking at the individual elements that make up any fully staged scene. Your first consideration when it comes to staging is, obviously, to make sure that there's logic of action to your scene—that the audience can make sense of what's happening. Your next consideration is how to stage the drama with maximum impact. How you balance these two considerations will largely define your cinematic style.

Point of View—Whose Is It?

WHEN FILMMAKERS REFER to point of view, they don't literally mean what a character sees (though this may involve a shot or two); they mean how a character is experiencing particular events. For example, you could tell a tragic love story by shooting most of the movie from the woman's angle, or you could tell the story from the perspective of her disapproving parents, or from a more detached, storyteller's point of view (also known as the omniscient POV). There are many options. One of your most important jobs as the director is to decide whose point of view to favor. Your decisions will dictate how you compose a shot, where you place your camera and actors, and how you edit a scene.

Many times the plot will clearly tell you whose point of view to favor. For example, if you have a stalker spying on a young woman, logic pretty much requires that you shoot much of the scene from the stalker's perspective. However, other times, it won't be so obvious. What if the woman, for example, is aware that she's being stalked and is secretly plotting to turn the tables? Now it's her scene as well, and you'll have to think harder about how to stage it. Of course, you can change point of view from character to character as required by the drama. Your challenge is to know when to do so and when to stay with a character so the audience can share his or her experiences.

Camera Placement

THERE ARE TWO KINDS of point of view: subjective and objective. A subjective point of view connects us to a character and tends to personally involve us in what she is doing, feeling, etc. For example, if you shoot over a boxer's shoulder while he's fighting, you put the audience in his shoes, so to speak. The audience is on the boxer's side of the fight and identifies with him. An objective point of view is more detached. In the boxing example, the camera would be placed at ringside or in another "neutral" position, and the point of view would not favor a particular character (see Figure 8.1).

When deciding where to place your camera, sightlines can be very instructive. These are basically the invisible lines between the main characters of a scene, as illustrated in Figure 8.2. In this diagram, a man and woman are having an argument while a child looks on. The major sightline is between the man and woman, but there are two other sightlines in the scene—one between the man and child, and one between the woman and child. Each line suggests a camera position.

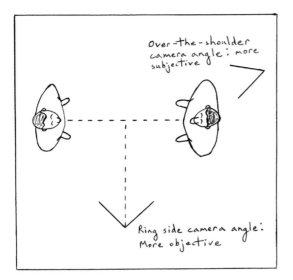

Figure 8.1

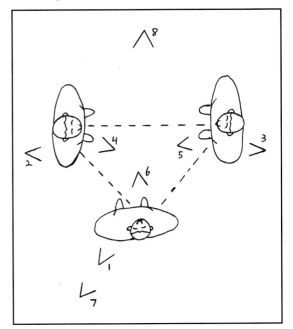

Figure 8.2

Figures 8.3 to 8.10 show how you might shoot the scene. Each photo corresponds to a camera angle indicated in Figure 8.2. As you can see, some angles are close and subjective as if viewed by one of the characters. Some are medium shots showing two people and suggest a neutral, storyteller's perspective. And a couple show more of an outsider's point of view covering all three characters.

Figure 8.3

Figure 8.4

Figure 8.5

Figure 8.6

Figure 8.7

Figure 8.9

Figure 8.8

Figure 8.10

Positioning Your Actors

HOW YOUR ACTORS are positioned in relation to each other in the frame can tell the audience a lot. Returning to the example of the arguing couple, if you show the child who's watching them in the same frame with the woman, it suggests a certain alliance between the two, that perhaps they're on the same side. On the other hand, if you show the man and woman in the same frame but the child separated in a close-up, it suggests she is cut off, perhaps alone.

There are a 1,001 other things you can do as a filmmaker to help an audience interpret a scene in a particular way. How your actors are lit, for example, can dramatically impact the mood of a scene. The dismal light of a gray, overcast day falling on someone's face can greatly intensify gloominess. So can carefully placed props and set dressing in the foreground and background, such as old decaying furniture, faded yellow curtains, etc. The effect is intensified if you can find a way to have your actors engage these elements in some way and bring them into focus for the audience, such as someone sitting down on an old, decrepit couch and perhaps touching the fabric. As long as your characters' actions are dramatically justified, the sky's the limit. There are no rules, only your instincts and creativity.

Lenses and Perspective

THE HUMAN EYE TAKES in a field of almost 180 degrees. In other words, we see a lot—much more than the widest camera lens. The limited view allowed by cameras has a big impact on how filmmakers set up their shots. Actors, for example, are often required to stand much closer to each other than they would in real life, so that they can be seen in the frame. And objects are often "cheated" together or apart to create the needed effect.

As for physical movements, it may be necessary to slow them down so that the camera captures them clearly. These little tricks, done properly, go unnoticed by the audience. Shooting some screen tests will help you make the right choices. Also, study classical paintings, photographs, etc. to develop your eye in this area, and take some experimental photos with a variety of lenses. If you're only using the zoom lens that came with your camera, experiment with a variety of focal length settings. Prime lenses, on the other hand, have one fixed focal length and are attached to your camera as required by your plans. Examples include wide-angle lenses and telephoto lenses.

When it comes to picking the right lens size (or focal length setting), many people feel intimidated, but the truth is, you don't need to be an expert in optics to use lenses effectively.

Simply explaining them in layman's terms can help you grasp the basic principles. To start, there are normal lenses, which, of course, give a normal perspective close to what we see with the human eye, as shown in Figure 8.12. On either side of "normal," there are wider perspectives and closer perspectives.

Wider views obviously allow the viewer to "see" a lot and have deep focus, meaning virtually everything in the frame, from foreground to background, is in sharp focus (see Figure 8.11). This can be useful at times when you want to compose large shots full of detail that stress a sense of distance. Wide-angle lenses also operate well when you're shooting in low light conditions. And wide angles are more steady than close perspectives when you're shooting handheld. However, wide-angle shots can sometimes include too much detail and drown out your subject. They also tend to distort people and objects that get too close to the camera.

Closer perspectives, as shown in Figure 8.13, give you a much narrower depth of field—in other words, a smaller area in which things are in focus. They're very good for isolating actors in the frame and keeping background details soft and out of focus. They're also very useful if you want to flatten or compress the sense of distance between foreground and background. The downsides of close shots include difficulty keeping moving subjects in focus and considerable unsteadiness when shooting handheld.

Figure 8.11

Figure 8.12

Figure 8.13

Moving Your Camera

WHEN CONSIDERING CAMERA moves, aside from simple pans or tilts, always remember that they're tough to pull off under the best of circumstances. Even if you have an ultra-experienced crew with all the necessary equipment, camera moves take a lot of time to set up and choreograph. And time is not your friend on a low-budget shoot.

In my experience, most novice directors love to plan complicated moves involving dollies, cranes, etc. because it makes them feel professional and "cool." However, they quickly learn that the cost of such an ego stroke can be enormous and literally destroy a budget and shooting schedule. I urge you to be brutally honest with yourself when planning camera moves and decide whether you truly need them to tell your story. Are they *really* dramatically justified? Sometimes the answer will be yes; but, more often, it will be no, and that's when you must have the courage to be simple.

I can assure you that almost all big-budget camera moves can be achieved in simpler, cheaper ways (such as pans, tilts, handhelds) without sacrificing dramatic impact. As I've suggested several times, study the masters—the great directors—and how they shot scenes similar to the ones you're considering. Also, think hard about the following aspects when deciding where to position your camera and whether to move it:

▶ **Point of View.** Through which character's point of view will the audience best experience the scene? For example, if you have a scene at a busy trade show, it probably wouldn't make sense to restrict your camera to fixed shots on a tripod. A smart choice would be to show much of the scene from the perspective of someone attending the show and moving through the crowd from display to display. On the other hand, if your scene takes place at a funeral, you probably want a calmer, steadier camera, regardless of whose point of view you choose. The key is to always ask yourself whose perspective should the audience be sharing most?

▶ **The Nature of the Scene.** Is it an energetic scene involving improvised performances, or is it a composed, controlled scene that is tightly scripted? If it's a kinetic scene with a lot of ad libbing, you might want to consider a moving camera to support the energy and capture the performances.

▶ **Background.** What role does it play in your scene? How can it be used to maximize the drama? For example, let's say you have a professional baseball player who has just lost the biggest game of his life, and he's sitting on the bench hanging his head. In the background the team mascot is dancing around with a big smile. This is a wonderful counterpoint to really drive home the player's pain. It enhances and adds dimension to your scene.

▶ **Location.** What does the location offer to improve your scene? How can you position or move your camera to include the useful part(s) of a location in your shot? For example, a popular way to visually reinforce a character's feeling of imprisonment or entrapment is to shoot him through bars, a fence, or some other confining object.

▶ **Zoom or Dolly?** When you zoom in on a character or object, you don't actually get closer to it; it only appears that you do because the entire image gets magnified. When you dolly in on someone or something, you are physically getting closer to it, and therefore your perspective actually changes, as it would in real life. There is an important difference between the two moves. As a director, you must decide which kind of shot best supports the drama of your scene. Put another way, do you really need a difficult dolly shot for scene X, or will a slow, careful zoom equally achieve what you want?

▶ **Character Relationships.** As I mentioned earlier in this chapter, you should always concentrate on how to best position your actors in relation to each other in the frame. This directly affects how you position your camera. Sometimes you'll find that a camera move is called for to effectively capture two or more characters that you want in the same shot—perhaps to suggest a union or common goal, attitude, etc.

Summary

▶ When staging a scene, your first priority is to ensure that there's logic of action, that it will make sense to an audience.

▶ Always be conscious of point of view. Which character's perspective should you favor to maximize dramatic impact?

▶ How you position your actors in relation to each other can tell the audience a great deal, as can how your actors relate to their location, props, etc.

▶ Educate yourself on the basic principles of lens use.

▶ Always remember that camera moves are tough to pull off and can eat up valuable time. Have the courage to be simple.

▶ When deciding where to position your camera, carefully consider

- Whose point of view you should favor
- The tone of the scene—is it tense or relaxed, energetic or calm?
- Background—how can it be used to maximum effect?
- Location and props—what do they offer to improve your scene?
- Movement—does moving your camera add to the drama?
- Character relationships—what's the most effective way to position your actors in relation to each other?

Directing Your
Cast and Crew

I'M NOT GOING TO LIE TO YOU. Directing a movie, regardless of its size, is an extremely stressful experience, even under the best of circumstances. Not to say there aren't moments of great excitement and gratification, but for the most part you will be pulled in one hundred different directions every day, juggling both your actors' and crew's needs while getting little if any sleep. It becomes the ultimate endurance test.

Consider, for example, shooting a simple take of two actors having a conversation. As you're intensely studying the actors' performances, you suddenly hear a noisy garbage truck outside. You're convinced it's ruining your sound recording, but you don't want to risk yelling, "cut!" because the actors are performing beautifully. Suddenly, you notice that the camera framing is off a little. You're not sure how it happened. Did your cameraman screw up? Can you salvage the shot anyway? Then one of your actors takes it upon himself to improvise his lines and actions without your prior consent. Your mind starts racing: "Can I still cut this scene together?" Before you know it, the take is over and everyone is looking to you for a reaction. Did you like it? Of course, you're speechless.

Communication and Your Authority

T HE MOST IMPORTANT directing skill is communication (see Figure 9.1). Though this may seem like a skill anyone can master, it is, in practice, very difficult and challenging. The director must be able to clearly communicate what he wants to dozens (and sometimes hundreds) of different artists and technicians—quickly and with complete confidence. Not so easy when you're exhausted and facing hundreds of questions a day. Nonetheless, you are the boss, the head coach, and you must never let this fact come into question. You dictate the team's strategy and give marching orders to all players. Of course, you should always be open to your players' advice, as they will no doubt bring invaluable experience and ideas to your movie. But at the end of the day, your word is final.

Figure 9.1

Actors First

YOUR ACTORS ARE YOUR first priority, no ifs, ands, or buts. You are their only audience on a movie shoot, and they desperately need your feedback after every take —intelligent feedback, not empty words like, "Nice work!" Despite everything else swirling around you, it's crucial that you concentrate on your actors every time the camera rolls. This may sound obvious—and easy—but it's not. You must focus on many performance aspects at the same time and make many mental notes on the fly:

▶ Are your lead actors "present" and relating to each other in a truthful manner? If not, where exactly are they slipping?

▶ Are they "on script" or ad libbing in a way you dislike? Again, where exactly?

▶ What about their blocking and body language?

▶ How are your supporting actors performing? What about your extras?

When the scene's over, you must immediately communicate all your thoughts in a clear and concise manner. Like I said, not so easy. What makes it *easier,* is delegating as much as you can that is not actor-related to your department heads or "keys," like your director of photography (if you have one), production manager, assistants, etc. Obviously, you need to choose these people very carefully and trust that they know what they're doing and understand and support your vision.

Managing Your Actors' Tensions

A GOOD IDEA BEFORE starting any shoot is to gather all your cast and crew together for dinner or drinks—usually a night or two before production begins. This tends to break the ice for everyone and also creates a sense of community and teamwork. I threw a potluck dinner the night before starting production on my first feature, *River Rats*, which allowed several cast and crew members to meet for the first time in a relaxed, social setting. The next morning as we began shooting I could clearly see the positive effect, as many of these people were already behaving as close colleagues, even friends (see Figure 9.2).

You should also find a few moments shortly before commencing production to warn your inexperienced actors that shooting a movie is a slow and often tedious process. Given all the time required to set up lights, equipment, block rehearsals, etc. you may only shoot a few minutes of footage per day. Encourage your actors to bring some books, music (with headphones, of course), DVDs, etc. to the set so they can occupy themselves during periods of waiting.

Figure 9.2
Dave Watson and Paul Lewandowski horsing around like buddies on the set of *River Rats*. This photo was taken the day after they first met at our cast and crew dinner, where they were able to "break the ice" and get to know each other.

Since most actors are extremely nervous and uneasy on the first day of a shoot, it's a good idea to schedule your least demanding scenes first. This allows your performers to warm up and get comfortable before the "heavy" stuff begins. You should also cater to your actors more than usual during the early days of a shoot—again, to alleviate their tensions and insecurities. Show them your appreciation for even small achievements—ideally, in the presence of their fellow actors and crew. This will work wonders for confidence and morale.

Be Organized

A S I'VE STRESSED, knowing what you want from top to bottom is imperative if you are to be successful and respected by your actors and crew. This requires intense advanced preparation. To start, typed call sheets (as shown in Figure 9.3) should be ready the night before every shooting day, as should any storyboards or floor plans that need to be distributed to cast and crew.

Your shooting plans for the day should already be thoroughly worked out with your DP, and all necessary costumes and props should be ready to go. The list goes on and on. You must be on top of everything and have answers for anything because your people will regularly test and challenge your leadership; it's human nature. When they see that you can't be shaken, you'll have their trust and respect, and your production will run smoothly.

SAMPLE CALL SHEET

"MOVIE XYZ"

8:00 AM

Producers: _____ Date: _____

Director: _____ Crew Call: _____

First AD: _____ Shooting Call: _____

Set/Scene Description	Day/Night	Scenes	Required Cast	Number of Pages
Int. Joe's Bedroom	Day	10	1,2	2
Ext. Bill's Backyard	Night	52, 53	1,2,3	3 1/8
etc.				
etc.				
etc.				
				Total Pages

Cast	Characters	Makeup Call	Set Call	Remarks
1. Steve Smith	Joe	9:00 AM	9:30 AM	None
2. Chris Jones	Elliot	9:00 AM	9:30 AM	
3. Andy Ackerson	Bill	9:00 AM	9:30 AM	

Crew	Call			
Writer/Director	8:00 AM			
Director of Photography	8:00 AM			
Sound Recordist	8:00 AM			
Production Assistants	8:00 AM			

Special Notes:

Props: 5 wine glasses, table and chairs

Makeup: for bad rash on Bill

Effects: rain using several garden hoses

Figure 9.3

Directing Actors on Set

AFTER WEEKS, IF NOT months, of preparation, you're now only minutes away from actually shooting your movie and directing your actors. As the crew sets up the first shot, take your cast aside and rehearse. Remind your actors where they are in the story (as you are likely shooting out of sequence) and what emotional condition their characters are in. Use your instincts to determine whether the actors should rehearse their dialogue, as you don't want to drain their energies before the camera rolls. Sometimes having them run lines at "half-speed" helps, sometimes not. Call it as you feel it. Once the crew has set up the shot, call for silence as everyone takes their positions. This allows your actors to focus and get "in the zone." Once they signal that they're ready, roll camera and call, "Action!" (See Figure 9.4.)

Generally speaking, only the director can call "cut!" Sometimes your DP or sound recordist will do so if they run into a technical issue that ruins the take. Actors, on the other hand, should always complete a flawed take until you decide to stop it, as they may not be aware that a "happy accident" has occurred which has improved the scene. If you decide that another take is necessary, go quickly, before your cast's energy and focus disappear. Briefly tell each actor what you expect, then roll the camera.

Figure 9.4

Often, actors themselves will be dissatisfied with their performances and ask to do another take. If time isn't an issue you should always indulge them. That said, some actors will take this too far, and you'll have to kindly put your foot down and insist that the last take was fine and that you're moving on. This kind of "director veto" is inevitable on a movie shoot, and you should be prepared for it. You're the general and that often means asserting your authority. It also means pushing your actors to deliver the best they have—and more—because it's all too easy to accept what they give as "good enough." Your job is not to be comfortable or popular, it's to lead and inspire. If this creates friction with certain cast and crew, so be it. All will be forgiven when the film is finished and successful (see Figure 9.5).

Figure 9.5
Cathy Reddy (left) taking a moment to get into character on the set of *River Rats* as we wait in silence.

Firing Up a Stale Scene

AS YOU SHOOT TAKE after take of a scene, you'll sometimes find it sinking into staleness or a certain mediocrity that you want to shake up. One thing you can do when this happens is to take an actor aside and suggest a small change unknown to the other players—for example, a slight change in dialogue or action. When they perform the scene again, the change creates some tension that puts everyone back on their toes and reignites the scene.

Alternatively, you can surprise all the actors by verbally suggesting a change in the middle of shooting a scene. For example, calling out, "Bill, she's lying and making a fool of you! Don't take that!" Your voice instantly gets your actor thinking and feeling in a new way; it sparks his imagination—and the scene. However, if you have never done this kind of side-coaching with your actors before, it may throw them completely and shatter the scene. Since it's an effective method, I suggest you occasionally use it in rehearsals, so that your actors come to expect it.

Dealing with Criticism

WHEN IT COMES TO CRITICISM you receive from your actors regarding your directing style or the script, always have an open mind. Actors are creative artists and often have ideas that never even occurred to you. If they have some constructive criticism, keep your ego in check and listen carefully. If you like their ideas, credit them. A smart director will always take intelligent suggestions from anyone on his team. However, if you find that an actor's criticism is useless to your film or even destructive, you must say so— and back it up with a clear explanation.

If a crew member has some criticism, he should always express it to you privately. The moment your actors think they're being directed by a committee, your authority goes out the window, and so does your movie. If one of your crew members voices criticism on set, give him a warning. If he does it again, fire him and never look back.

If an actor approaches a crew member looking for opinions on his quality of work, the crew member (per your prior warning) should only be supportive—which is what most actors want anyway. Under no circumstances should crew get into critical discussions with cast members, as this is solely the director's territory.

Taking Care of Your People

A S YOUR SHOOT WEARS ON, an exhausted cast and crew is almost inevitable—and yet you must do everything in your power to protect against exhaustion. When people get tired, they get irritable, sloppy, and their work suffers. You can guard against fatigue by first making sure that your shooting schedule is not unrealistic—i.e., virtually impossible to complete in the time you have. Many low-budget shoots have outrageous schedules. Don't let yours be one of them. Be conservative so things get done right.

When shooting, give your people 10-minute breaks every few hours. You must also take special care of their creature comforts. Have food and drink available at all times—and don't skimp, get the good stuff. Make sure there are plenty of places to sit and that there's easy access to clean bathrooms. If you're shooting in cold conditions, make sure there is sufficient heat. Hot conditions, sufficient A/C. You get the idea. At the end of each shooting day, make an effort to personally thank as many people as possible for their hard work. This kind of TLC goes a long way in ensuring a happy and productive film company.

Communicating with Your Crew

THOUGH YOU DON'T NEED to be an expert in each technical area handled by your crew, you should try to have at least a basic understanding of each technician's craft (see Figures 9.6 and 9.7), so that you communicate your needs clearly and effectively. Again, it's about doing your homework well in advance: reading the right books, talking to professionals, experimenting on your own, etc.

Figure 9.6
A small crew setting up for a shot.

Figure 9.7
A professional sound recordist operating his equipment on set.

By the time shooting starts, all crew members will have read your script and given their feedback as it relates to their areas of expertise. You, in turn, will have given them clear, specific instructions for each shooting day that cannot be misunderstood or misinterpreted (see Figure 9.8).

When it comes to dealing with your crew on set, delegating is extremely important, so that you can concentrate on your actors and the film. If you have a DP or AD (assistant director), he or she should communicate your directions to the rest of the crew as often as possible.

Figure 9.8
My director of photography, Mike Tien, and I filming a scene for *River Rats*. Before production began, I made sure to read up on shooting black-and-white 16mm film. I also talked to experts and I shot some tests, so that I could clearly and confidently communicate with Mike about camera, film stock, lighting, etc.

Every time your crew sets up a new shot, it's important that you look through the camera's viewfinder (or at the video monitor connected to the camera) to confirm the composition meets your expectations. When a shot involves a moving camera or character action, it's your job to walk the actors through the shot, freezing them at the right points so that your camera crew can see what you have in mind and make sure they're covering it all (see Figure 9.9).

Figure 9.9
Shooting an action scene on *River Rats*. By delegating all technical responsibilities to my crew, I was able to work intensively with my actors and focus on the drama.

Measuring Progress and Quality

THE GREAT THING ABOUT shooting on video is that you can watch a take on the monitor and immediately see what you're getting. You can also play back and review a take as many times as you'd like. This kind of analysis, however, is best kept until the end of each shooting day when you will review all of your day's footage (called *dailies* or *rushes*) with your crew. Actors should not be invited to dailies, as they often dislike seeing themselves on screen and may decide to change their performances in ways you don't support.

During these daily screenings you'll be able see the level of quality you're getting—in performances, drama, picture, sound, etc. You'll also be able to see if an important shot was forgotten or botched in some way. This kind of early detection is critical, as you can easily reshoot or pick up a shot the next day since you still have your sets in place and your cast and crew assembled.

Though you may be able to monitor the dramatic quality of your movie by simply watching your rushes every night, the best way to do it is to assemble your raw footage into a scene as soon as possible. By viewing a scene in its edited form, you can see a great deal more, even if it's only a rough cut. Any inconsistencies in acting, lighting, composition, sound, or continuity now show up early enough to make fixes. Your challenge, of course, will be to find a skilled and affordable editor to assemble your dailies, since you will surely have no time or energy to do it yourself during production. If you're not able to find someone, I strongly suggest that you throw back 10 cups of coffee and take a couple of hours to roughly assemble your scenes. It's that important.

Summary

▶ Directing a movie is very tough. Prepare yourself.

▶ You are the boss. The best way to assert your authority is to be well prepared and organized, and to communicate clearly.

▶ Actors are your first priority. Their work will largely determine whether your film is a success or failure.

▶ Rehearse with your actors every chance you get.

▶ Educate yourself on ways to fire up a stale scene.

▶ Demand that your crewmembers express any criticism privately—and only to you.

▶ Try to have at least a basic understanding of every crewmember's craft, so that you can communicate with them clearly and effectively.

▶ Review all of each day's footage (dailies or rushes) at the end of each shooting day. Determine what needs to be reshot or picked up.

▶ Try to roughly assemble your scenes as early as possible, to further detect any inconsistencies in acting, lighting, and sound.

Post-Production

S O, YOUR FILM IS SHOT and you've spent some cash, possibly a serious amount. Now, with whatever you have left, you move on to post-production and finish your movie—hopefully, after a long rest, as I'm sure you're completely wiped from your shoot. The good news is, post-production is a very logical and organized process, unlike shooting, which is usually controlled chaos, at best. In post, you simply move forward one step at a time.

Given your budget, I'm assuming that you will be editing the film yourself, most likely on a computer-based system like Final Cut Pro or Adobe Premiere. If you have an experienced editor helping you, consider yourself very lucky; but it still behooves you to learn everything you can about the different phases of post-production outlined in this chapter, not only to communicate intelligently with your editor but also so that you can take the driver's seat if the need arises (and trust me, it often does).

Picture Editing

A S THE DIRECTOR, you've been concerned about your film as a whole from the beginning, always conscious of the "big picture" when evaluating script, performances, and so forth. It's crucial that this mindset continue now into post-production, as your editing style should serve your overall vision and be consistent with the tone you've already established. Any flashy, music-video editing, for example, better fit your movie or it's going to stick out like a sore thumb.

Your first step in picture editing is to put together a "first assembly," a long, crude version of your film that is faithful to the script. The first assembly does not concern itself with length or balance. In fact, it usually consists of master shots with very little cutting, close-ups, etc. You just want to put together your scenes to get a sense of your film as a whole and get an idea of what further development is required.

You may, for example, see that some performances need work, or that a scene is falling flat and may need to be removed. Whatever you see, it's important that you forget what your original intentions were. They're irrelevant at this point.

Figure 10.1
A typical home computer editing setup.

You have to work with what you have and be open to new ideas and approaches. Also, prepare yourself to be disappointed, possibly even depressed. Watching a first assembly is usually very difficult, as just about everything is in its crudest form possible: the performances, the pacing, there's no music or sound effects, no titles, no smooth transitions, etc. I urge you not to despair. Every filmmaker on the planet goes through this process. Rest easy in the fact that your film will gradually improve over the coming months into something wonderful.

When watching your first assembly, make sure there are no interruptions. Lock the door, kill the lights, and watch from beginning to end without stopping and without taking notes. Your focus should only be on the screen. If possible, have your editor or a trusted confidante watch it with you. After the screening, discuss your thoughts, then watch the film again, this time taking notes. Here are some problems (and solutions) that you may run into:

▶ **The acting is weak in certain sections.** Some help is available in further editing, especially dialogue editing. With today's digital technology, you can literally piece together a line by using single words from several different takes. This is extremely tedious and time-consuming, obviously, but in a pinch it can seamlessly produce great dialogue and save your butt. There is also the option of automatic dialogue replacement (A.D.R.), which I'll cover later.

▶ **The writing is weak in certain sections.** You may have to cut scenes out entirely or shorten them. Another option (budget permitting) is to rewrite the faulty scenes and reshoot them.

▶ **Some scenes are repetitive or do not advance the story.** Have the courage to kill them, even if they're your "darlings."

▶ **Some scenes drag or continue beyond a good ending point.** Again, have the courage to cut them down.

▶ **The drama is not escalating.** Sometimes simply rearranging scenes (or dropping them) will have an enormous impact on a film's momentum. Experiment with various arrangements, even ones that you feel are completely wrong. You may be pleasantly surprised.

Once you have identified all of your problem areas, prioritize them. Tackle the biggest problems first. For example, if you feel that your film's overall dramatic structure is weak, rearrange or drop scenes as you see fit—and do nothing else—then watch the entire film again.

One of the most common problems with amateur films is that they're too long and too slow. Even professional filmmakers are often guilty of painfully slow, self-indulgent movies. One solution is to decide early how long your film should be. From Day 1, for example, I knew that my second feature, *Alone With Her*, should be a lean 80-85 minute psychological thriller. This allowed me to get tough with any cuts of the film that were beyond this running time. We ultimately locked the film at a tight 81 minutes.

Basic Editing Techniques

WHEN EDITING, THERE are a few basic techniques you should be aware of—rules that have been developed over the past century that audiences have come to accept as part of the language of filmmaking.

▶ **Each cut should be dramatically motivated.** In other words, it should be organic to your scene and story, not simply a cut for the sake of movement, flash, etc. Cutting should also be "invisible," unless there's a good reason to draw attention to it. Edits should feel natural to the audience and go virtually unnoticed.

▶ **Cut on motion.** Cuts always look smoother when they happen during motion in the frame. For example, as a woman enters a room in a master shot, cut to a medium shot of the same woman still in motion (see Figures 10.2, 10.3, and the DVD for examples).

Figure 10.3

Figure 10.2

► **Use cutaways to solve continuity problems.** *Cutaways* are shots that aren't directly related to a scene but still fit and make sense. They're useful in acting as a bridge between shots that otherwise could not be cut together. For example, let's say you have a two-shot of a man and woman having a heated argument. The performances are amazing, but halfway through the scene one of your actors flubs a line for a few seconds before getting back on track. In this case, you might place a cutaway of their child watching in shock from the couch over the shot of the flubbed line, "clean up" the dialogue with sound editing, then return to the two-shot of the argument, as shown in Figures 10.4 to 10.6.

Figure 10.4

Figure 10.5

Figure 10.6

The Rough Cut and Beyond

THE NEXT CUT AFTER YOUR first assembly is the rough cut. This is a tighter, more refined version of your movie but one that still needs some major fine-tuning. As you did with your first assembly, you should address problems from largest to smallest. Questions to ask yourself include

1. Does the film stop too often to spoon-feed the audience important information or back-story?

2. If I cut some of these scenes, will the audience still be able to understand what's going on?

3. Does the film's drama escalate steadily?

4. Do my major characters develop over the course of the film in a believable and satisfying manner?

5. Is there a good balance between indoor and outdoor scenes, or does the film come off as suffocating and claustrophobic?

6. Can I further tighten certain scenes by starting them later and ending them earlier?

7. How strong is my ending?

Over the course of many weeks, your film will evolve through several versions to a "final cut." The danger you face as a director-editor is losing your objectivity as you watch the same footage over and over again. Everything starts to look the same. For that reason, you should take frequent breaks from the editing room to clear your head—ideally, every weekend so that you can come back with a relatively fresh perspective. Also, starting with the rough cut, you should show your movie to small groups of people whose tastes you respect, as their feedback can be invaluable.

Showing Your Work-In-Progress

BEFORE SHOWING YOUR FILM, explain to your audience that the movie is a work-in-progress and lacks the polish they've come to expect from commercial movies and TV—i.e., picture and sound quality will be raw, music will be spotty or non-existent, no titles, etc. After the viewing, listen carefully to what your audience says and remain quiet. Whatever you do, don't get defensive or try to explain what you intended. You want truthful feedback, which you will review later in private. Listening to criticism is a tough experience, so be strong and truly *listen*, taking notes—or better yet, recording the whole thing.

To get the most out of these screenings, you should have a list of questions prepared for the audience. All the major studios in Hollywood use professional research companies to conduct audience screenings, and these companies hand out very comprehensive and detailed questionnaires to audiences after each screening. You don't have to go that far, but you should direct the Q&A to your advantage. Some good questions to ask are

1. Did you feel the film was too long, too short, or just the right length?

2. What did you think of the ending?

3. Who was your favorite character and why?

4. Who was your least favorite character and why?

5. What was the movie about, in your opinion?

6. Was there anything in the movie that confused you or that was unclear?

7. How would you rate this movie on a scale of 1 to 10?

Of course, feel free to add more questions of your own to this list—whatever you find useful.

Once you've had time to absorb all the feedback, return to the cutting room and get to work—but before rushing to fix anything, consider carefully the number of people that reported a particular problem. If it was only two out of twenty, you may not have to change anything. On the other hand, if 12 out of 20 report the same problem, I strongly suggest addressing it.

You may also run into a situation where 10 different people identify 1- different problems. This is where your confidence and personal convictions come into play. Always trust your instincts and stay true to your vision. Keep in mind that when people are put in a position to judge your film, they will often manufacture criticism if none comes to mind. In other words, they anxiously want to contribute and may spit out whatever half-baked idea pops into their head. So be careful.

A final note on editing: it's often a long, difficult process filled with trial and error. You will frequently doubt yourself and may even think that you have a piece of crap on your hands. Don't despair. All this is normal. The vast majority of movies come to life in the editing room.

Sound Editing

THE SOUND IN A MOVIE often goes unnoticed. It's taken for granted by audiences—unless it's bad. Then, boy, do people take notice. The truth is, poor sound can destroy a movie. Consider a simple scene involving a man walking into his garage, getting into his car, and pulling out. The sound effects in this scene would include the man's footsteps, the car door opening and closing, the engine starting, the automatic garage door opening, and the sounds of outside life and traffic pouring in. Of course, this is just a small sampling; there would be many more sounds that add significant depth to the images.

Creatively speaking, sound editing is a treat for a director. The smart use of sound can vividly bring out moods and emotions, set an atmosphere, and can even transform a weak performance into a great one. Sound is half your movie, and you must use it to the fullest. Even the lack of small sound effects that you may think are meaningless can make your movie feel somehow incomplete or amateurish.

As with picture editing, the ideal is to have an experienced sound editor at your side, but without this kind of help you can manage just fine by learning to operate your own system. The good news, again, for the low-budget filmmaker is that most desktop systems can now edit and mix sound in a fairly decent manner. These systems show graphic representations of all your sounds on your computer screen and show where each sound begins and ends. This makes it quite easy to cut, paste, and manipulate your dialogue, music, and sound effects as you wish.

Dialogue

THE FIRST THING YOU should focus on is your dialogue, cleaning up any imperfections. You can do this without watching the film's visuals. Just listen carefully to the dialogue tracks and cut out any hissing, clicks, pops, noise pollution, etc. whenever someone isn't speaking. You can fill in the blank spots with room tone (also known as ambient sound) that you recorded on location. It's crucial that you make these recordings on location because they're very difficult to find or produce after production. For example, on my first movie, we shot many scenes in an old, damp cellar with a very low ceiling. The room tone in this cellar was very unique and, had we not cleanly recorded it, we would have had a hell of a time finding its equivalent during editing. The same holds true for many exterior locations we used. Therefore, before leaving any shooting location, make sure you (or your sound recordist) call for one full minute of silence so that room tone/ambient sound can be cleanly recorded.

During editing, you may notice that some lines of dialogue need to be redone. Inserting new dialogue is called dubbing, or A.D.R. (automatic dialogue replacement). On professional films, this is done in a studio, but you can easily pull it off with a simple mike plugged into your computer. During this process, your actor (who you'll have to bring back) watches the part of film you want to fix and repeats his dialogue at the right moment. He'll probably have to do several takes, as it's tricky exactly syncing a voice with lips.

When all your dialogue is in place, you'll want to equalize it, which means raising and lowering it to get a good volume level throughout.

Sound Effects and Foley

TODAY, MOST SOUND EDITORS (even the part-timers editing in their basements) have big effects libraries—hundreds, if not thousands, of sounds they've collected over the years and saved digitally. If you're working with an editor then you're set; he can insert a myriad of sounds (at your direction) into your film and enrich it big time. If you don't have an editor, there are all kinds of CDs you can buy online that contain every sound effect imaginable, including storms, weapons, crowds, traffic, etc.

If for some reason you can't find the effect you're looking for in a library, there's always the option of *foley*—which means creating the sound. This is usually done by a foley artist who performs various sounds like footsteps, rustling clothes, punches, etc. on a special stage while watching the film on a screen. On your budget, you'll probably have to do it yourself (perhaps with the help of some friends) with a simple audio recorder—but so what? Chances are you'll have a great time creating the effects you need. And be creative! For example, you can play with any number of home tools to simulate the sound of a clicking gun or a sword being pulled out. As for punches to the face, just take some whacks at a piece of raw meat. A monster's roar: make several recordings of different barking dogs and mix them together on your computer, playing with the levels, etc. until you have something truly unique. Once again, you are only limited by your imagination.

Music and Score

IMAGINE SOME OF YOUR favorite movies without any music whatsoever. With the rarest exceptions, they fall flat. That's because music is one of the most important components of cinema. It establishes mood, intensifies drama, foreshadows, and can act as glue, connecting scenes and shots that would otherwise seem to have no relation. On a low-budget film, music can be a bona fide life-saver, transforming weak scenes into strong ones and smoothing out, if not completely disguising, any "wrinkles" in your film. That said, be very careful when selecting music for your movie, as novice filmmakers often make big mistakes in this area.

The first thing you should be aware of is music clearances. If you plan to show your film commercially (i.e., publicly screen it in any way), you must get formal permission to use any music created within the last 75 years. This costs money—truckloads of it, especially if you're talking about popular music. And don't think that classical music composed hundreds of years ago by the likes of Beethoven, Mozart, etc. is fair game. It's not, unless the recording that you want was created over 75 years ago. If you don't plan to show your film commercially and simply want to entertain family and friends, or use the film as a work sample to show potential employers, then by all means use whatever music your heart's set on.

If you're aiming for a bigger audience and ticket sales of some sort, you have basically three options:

▶ **Create and record the music yourself.**

▶ **Hire a composer who is looking for film experience and willing to work for pennies and a screen credit that says, "Music By."**

▶ **Use stock music that has already been "pre-cleared." This music can be bought online and is quite cheap, but obviously mediocre, at best, and sometimes downright awful.**

Mixing

SOUND MIXING, as the term suggests, is the process that brings all your film's sounds together into one unified soundtrack. On big-budget films, mixing is performed by several technicians in an expensive studio, and the process can take anywhere from a week to months. As you're most likely completing your film on your home computer, you'll have to mix the film yourself using whatever editing software you've chosen.

For the sake of simplicity, group all your sounds into three tracks: dialogue, music, and effects. This will allow you to raise and lower each track with relative ease as you put everything together. Generally speaking, only one sound should dominate a scene. For example, during a heated argument between two characters, dialogue would obviously be the dominant sound, with background noise and any music playing subordinate roles. An action scene like a car chase, on the other hand, might very well have pulse-pounding music as the dominant sound. There are no hard and fast rules, of course; like most aspects of filmmaking it's about following your instincts. You may find that the order of importance for sounds in a scene changes from minute to minute, requiring you to fade up the music to the foreground at one point, then quickly bring it down only seconds later so that dialogue can take a lead role.

A final note on mixing: be sure to save and back up your work often. I can't tell you how many horror stories I've heard over the years of filmmakers losing weeks of work because their computers crashed and they didn't have up-to-date backups. You will be investing many days of painstaking work into your mix. Always protect your work.

Titles

ON A LOW-BUDGET film, in particular, it's imperative that you credit everyone who worked for you in the titles, as most people probably worked for free or next to nothing. By acknowledging these people in your film's titles, you are giving them the ultimate thanks; you are immortalizing their contributions on celluloid (or videotape).

When preparing your titles, double- and triple-check that you have the correct spelling of everyone's name and that you haven't forgotten anybody. Also, be sure to confirm what role each person played. Regarding the sequence of credits, your film should open with its title, then go to actors, production designer, composer, editor, director of photography, producer, writer, and director last. If you want an ego stroke, you can also place your name right before the opening title with "A Film By Joe Blow" or "A Joe Blow Picture." Whatever you do, make sure your opening titles don't run too long, or you'll bore the hell out of your audience. As a general rule, keep each title on screen for only 2-3 seconds. Experiment, of course, but keep things moving.

The order of your end titles should be as follows: actors, production manager, assistant director, director of photography, camera crew, lighting crew, sound crew, art crew, editors, post-production personnel, any facilities that were used, music credits, special thanks you want to give to friends, family, etc. and your copyright notice.

Of course, these are only guidelines. As an independent filmmaker, you have the freedom to bend (or break) the rules as you see fit. I hope this freedom along with my humble advice has allowed you to fully indulge your talents and create a movie that you're not only proud of, but that truly entertains. So gather your friends, pop some corn, dim the lights... and cross your fingers!

Figure 10.7

Summary

► Always be conscious of the "big picture" when editing your movie.

► Make sure your editing style is consistent with the tone and content of your movie.

► Put together a "first assembly" to get a sense of your movie as a whole and to identify major problems. Don't despair. First assemblies almost always suck.

► Tackle the biggest problems first.

► Educate yourself on basic editing techniques.

► Put together a "rough cut." Once again, address problems from largest to smallest.

► As you work toward a "final cut," stay positive and take frequent breaks to preserve your objectivity.

► Starting with the rough cut, regularly show your movie to groups of people whose tastes you respect. Put your ego aside and carefully listen to their feedback. Always have questions prepared to get the most out of these screenings.

► Sound is half your movie. If it's poor, it can destroy your film.

► Focus on dialogue first, then move to sound effects and foley.

► Music can literally transform a movie. It's one of the most important components of cinema.

► If you plan to show your movie commercially, make sure you get all the necessary music clearances.

► When mixing your film, remember to always save and back up your work.

► Acknowledge the people who helped you in your movie's titles. Make sure you have the correct spelling of every person's name.

Glossary

Act

One of three underlying sections found in most screenplays.

Actor Release

A legal document that gives you the right to photograph/record your actors and exhibit the footage as you see fit.

AD

Assistant Director. A person who helps the director in the making of a movie.

ADR

Automatic Dialogue Replacement. The re-recording of dialogue after shooting.

Antagonist

The adversary or person opposed to the protagonist.

Callback

Calling back actors who have successfully passed the first round of auditions.

Character Arc

The change or evolution a character experiences over the course of a story.

Continuity
Consistency of actors' movements, lighting, sound, etc. between shots intended to match.

Coverage
The number of camera setups (and corresponding angles) used to film a scene and the amount of footage in a shot.

Crane Shot
A device supporting a camera, which can be raised or lowered during a shot.

CU
Close-up. A shot that tightly frames a person. Usually, a person's face.

Cutaway
A shot away from the central action of a scene. Very useful in acting as a bridge between shots that otherwise could not be edited together.

Dailies
Also known as rushes. All of a day's footage ready to be viewed.

Deep Focus
Virtually everything in the shot, from foreground to background, is in sharp focus.

Depth of Field
The depth of a shot that is in sharp focus.

Dolly
Generally, a buggy or cart on which you mount your camera to allow smooth tracking shots.

Dolly Shot
Smooth moving shot with the camera mounted on a cart or buggy.

DP
Director of Photography. The chief camera and lighting person on a movie, usually responsible for artistic decisions relating to the image.

Dutch Angle
When the camera is slanted at an angle to create a strange or imbalanced shot.

ECU
Extreme close-up. A shot that gets right in and shows extreme detail.

EXT
Exterior. Used to indicate a scene is outdoors.

EWS
Extreme wide shot. Often called an "establishing shot." Shows a subject's surroundings, such as a landscape, ocean, skyline, etc.

First Assembly
A long, crude version of a film that is faithful to the script.

Foley
Recreating sounds to picture.

High Angle
A shot that looks down at someone or something.

Improvisation
Also known as improv. Acting that purposely allows a spontaneous outcome.

Indicating
When an actor uses external, physical ways to show what his character is feeling.

INT
Interior. Used to indicate a scene is indoors.

Location Release
A legal document that gives you official permission to use property that isn't your own for the purpose of shooting your film.

Low Angle
A shot that looks up at someone or something.

Master Shot
A wide shot that shows most of the scene and characters.

Mixing
The process that brings all of a film's soundtracks together into one unified track.

MS
Medium shot. A shot from a medium distance.

Normal Lens
A lens that gives a normal perspective close to what is seen with the human eye.

On-the-nose
Painfully obvious and lacking subtlety/artistry. Usually referring to screenplay dialogue.

OSS
Over-the-shoulder shot. A shot of something or someone taken over the shoulder of another person.

Panning Shot
A horizontal camera movement where the camera moves left or right while on a stationary location, usually a tripod.

POV
Point-of-view shot. A shot showing what a character sees.

Presence
The emotional presence of an actor during a scene.

Protagonist
The central character of a story.

Pushing
When an actor feels a trace of real emotion inside himself and "pushes" it into existence, instead of trusting it to grow naturally and truthfully.

Read-through

When the director and his entire cast sit down together (usually for the first time), read the script out loud, and discuss it afterwards.

Room Tone

Naturally occurring atmospheric sound in any location. Recorded to fill in silent spots of a soundtrack. Also known as ambient sound.

Rough Cut

The next cut after a first assembly.

Rule of Thirds

Imagine a shot divided into horizontal and vertical thirds. The intersecting lines create four ideal points for positioning the shot's subject.

Screenplay

Formatted document of a film/video production containing dialogue and stage directions but no camera or editing instructions.

Script Breakdown

Dividing a screenplay into scenes, noting locations, required actors, props, etc. Essential in preparing a shooting script.

Shooting Script

A screenplay that has been revised to show numbered scenes and camera/editing instructions.

Steadicam

A special mechanical harness that holds the camera and virtually eliminates any shaking or unsteadiness.

Storyboard

A visual representation of a shot in diagram form.

Story Outline

A general description of your screenplay in bullet or point form.

Story Structure

The three-act structure of basic drama.

Tilting Shot

A vertical camera movement where your camera *tilts* up or down, again while fixed on a tripod.

TS

Two shot. A shot showing two characters in the frame.

WS

Wide shot. A shot in which the subject takes up the full frame.

Zooming Shot

Changing the focal length of a camera lens (usually by pressing a button) to magnify part of a shot.

Sample Script

ACADEMIC MISCONDUCT

Screenplay by
Eric Nicholas

Third Draft
March 11, 1999

When you look into the abyss,
the abyss also looks into you.

- Friedrich Nietzsche

1

FADE IN:

EXT. NORTHEASTERN UNIVERSITY - BOSTON, MASS. - DAY

THE CAMPUS. Late fall. An enclave of fast-paced student
activity set against picture postcard New England scenery.
Towering elms with breathtaking canopies of orange-red leaves.
Rich, manicured lawns. Modern and classic school buildings.

And STUDENTS. Hundreds of them -- from every walk of life --
swarming the campus streets and paths like mice in a maze, all
in pursuit of one thing: SUCCESS. CREDITS run...

ANGLE ON a monumental stone building, its busy MAIN ENTRANCE a
steady blur of passing faces, bodies, textbooks, backpacks,
briefcases, entering, exiting, finally pumping out:

TOMMY GREENE

21, handsome, all-American. Ambitious eyes masking a hint of
exhaustion, stress.

MOVING WITH TOMMY as he rushes down the steps and continues
his hectic day, a day like all the others -- too much to do,
too little time.

CAMPUS MONTAGE:

INT. LECTURE HALL
Tommy sitting among a crowd of students, diligently taking
notes as a PROFESSOR drones on...Hurrying out at the
conclusion, into:

INT. SCHOOL CAFETERIA
Sequestering himself at a quiet table. Studying hard. Taking
an occasional bite from a sandwich. Rolling his stiff neck,
overworked. He checks his watch. Dashes out.

INT. CLASSROOM
A test in progress. Tommy rivetted to his paper, concentrating
intensely, pen scrawling a-mile-a-minute. A PROFESSOR at the
front of the class writes <u>5 Minutes!</u> on the blackboard. Tommy
quickly completes his paper. Hands it in.

INT. LIBRARY
At a computer terminal. Tommy searching the database for a
case book, fingers hammering the keyboard, striking out every
time. Frustrated, he rushes out.

EXT. CAMPUS PATHS
Twilight now. Tommy jogs across campus toward a large brick
building, backpack bouncing at his side, heavy with books.

INT. DORM ROOM - TWILIGHT

Tommy enters and dashes straight for his closet, his roommate
STEVE FOX on the phone -- a dark, intense young man with
rugged good looks. Pinned to the bookshelf dividing their
room, a FRAMED PHOTO of the boys at a frat party, beer mugs in
hand, arms around each other. Best friends.

> STEVE (mutters into phone)
> Yeah...Look, I gotta jet, I work at
> seven...Right, call you later.

He hangs up, an air of disappointment about him. Tommy
hurriedly changing into some dress clothes.

> TOMMY
> Sorry I bailed -- had to drive all the
> way downtown to find that case book.
> How was class?

Steve crosses the room and tosses a booklet on Tommy's bed.

> TOMMY
> What's that?

> STEVE
> It's your midterm.
>   (off Tommy's look)
> I picked it up for you.

> TOMMY
> They're already marked?

He anxiously snatches the exam booklet and fixes on the cover
page. His face goes slack. A "C" circled in red ink under his
name. He stares blankly for a beat. Wearily shakes his head.

> TOMMY
> ...What did you get?

> STEVE
> Same. Class average was a D-plus.

> TOMMY (issues a deep sigh)
> Wonderful...my first "C" in ten
> years...

He tosses the exam on his bed, visibly distressed, and
continues to change.

> STEVE
> Look, how bad do you want it?

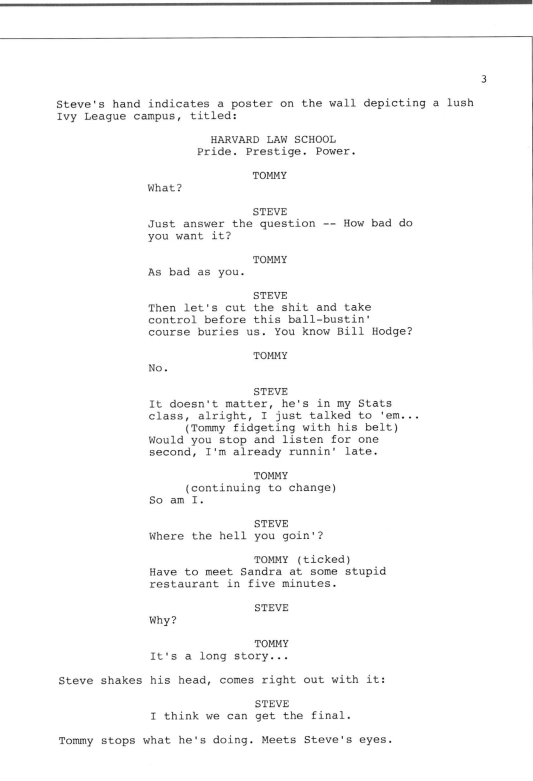

Steve's hand indicates a poster on the wall depicting a lush
Ivy League campus, titled:

> HARVARD LAW SCHOOL
> Pride. Prestige. Power.

> TOMMY
> What?

> STEVE
> Just answer the question -- How bad do
> you want it?

> TOMMY
> As bad as you.

> STEVE
> Then let's cut the shit and take
> control before this ball-bustin'
> course buries us. You know Bill Hodge?

> TOMMY
> No.

> STEVE
> It doesn't matter, he's in my Stats
> class, alright, I just talked to 'em...
> (Tommy fidgeting with his belt)
> Would you stop and listen for one
> second, I'm already runnin' late.

> TOMMY
> (continuing to change)
> So am I.

> STEVE
> Where the hell you goin'?

> TOMMY (ticked)
> Have to meet Sandra at some stupid
> restaurant in five minutes.

> STEVE
> Why?

> TOMMY
> It's a long story...

Steve shakes his head, comes right out with it:

> STEVE
> I think we can get the final.

Tommy stops what he's doing. Meets Steve's eyes.

                    TOMMY
          What are you talking about?

                    STEVE
          Just what I said. I think we can get
          the final exam.

                    TOMMY

          From who?

                    STEVE
          Beth Anderson.

                    TOMMY
          Who's Beth Anderson?

                    STEVE
          Our TA. Hodge says she's..."open" to
          financial persuasion, if you know what
          I mean.

                    TOMMY
          You wanna bribe her for the final...

He utters a dazed little laugh. Takes a seat on his bed,
starts tying his shoes.

                    STEVE
          She's done it before.

                    TOMMY

          With who?

                    STEVE
          Hodge's ex-girlfriend, two years ago.

Tommy shakes his head at the very idea.

                    STEVE
          Think about it -- A precedent's been
          set. It's not like we'd be approaching
          her with our pants down.

                    TOMMY
               (rises, grabs his jacket)
          I can't believe I'm hearing this.

                    STEVE
          Why are you bein' such a wuss!

                    TOMMY
          Look, if you wanna do it so bad, just
          do it, why do you need me?

5

                    STEVE
Because I can't raise three grand
alone.

                    TOMMY
Three grand!

                    STEVE
Whad'you expect, a buck fifty?

                    TOMMY (heads for the door)
I don't have time for this.

                    STEVE (pissed)
Fine, forget it. Take your fuckin' "C"
and go to Boston College.
          (off Tommy's reaction)
You think Harvard Law's gonna even
consider two assholes with "C"s in
English Lit? It's the most important
course we have!

                    TOMMY
          (with a lot more confidence
          than he feels)
We're not gonna get "C"s.

                    STEVE
We're not?

                    TOMMY
No -- 'cause we're gonna study our
asses off for the final.

                    STEVE
Oh Christ!
          (snatches Tommy's midterm,
          shakes it in the air)
And we didn't study hard for this? We
didn't study two fuckin' weeks for
this? A PHD couldn't score an "A" on
this goddamn midterm! You think the
final's gonna be any different?

                    TOMMY
The final won't be as hard.

                    STEVE
How the hell do you know!

                    TOMMY
Because if it is, the class average is
gonna be a D-plus -- which is totally
against school policy. The Dean'll end
up bell-curving the grades anyway!

                              STEVE
                    (takes a riled breath, then
                    cold, deliberate)
          Even if it's easier, which it won't
          be, thanks to this--
                    (the midterm)
          we need over ninety-five on the final,
          just to get an "A" in the course.
          Ninety-five percent.

                              TOMMY
          I know, it's gonna be tough.

                              STEVE
          So instead of quarantying yourself an
          "A", with no work whatsoever, you'd
          rather bust your ass for eight weeks,
          stick your finger in the dike and
          pray.

                         TOMMY (uncertain)
          Yeah...I would...

A silence between them. Tommy tenuously holding his ground at
the door, temptation flickering in his eyes. There's something
very powerful and intimidating about Steve that's almost
ensnaring him. Finally, he speaks, softly, his voice imbued
with shaky resolve:

                              TOMMY
          Look...I hear what you're saying...
          Seriously, I do...But I can't do this.
          I just can't. I'm sorry.
                    (beat)
          I gotta go...
                    (he opens the door)
          I'll talk to you tomorrow.

And he exits before Steve can press any further. Beat. And
Steve angrily SLAMS Tommy's closet door.

INT. FANCY RESTAURANT - DOWNTOWN BOSTON - NIGHT

A plush reception area, dark mahogany wood, a long oak bar.
Tommy enters and is met by the MAITRE D'.

                              TOMMY
          Hi, I'm Tommy Greene. I'm meeting--

                              MAITRE D'
          Yes, Mr. Greene. This way please.

He leads Tommy into the main dining room and--

                          BIG CROWD
            SURPRISE!!

Tommy is stunned by a cheering DINNER PARTY comprised of his
parents, his girlfriend SANDRA, and dozens of distinguished
guests. They all start into "Happy Birthday" as Sandra glides
to Tommy and gives him a big hug. She's an attractive
brunette, a cozy small-town feel about her.

                          SANDRA
            A week early, but definitely worth the
            look on your face.

Tommy laughs to himself as they ease into a kiss, whistles and
applause coming from the crowd. He joins the party, embracing
his parents, shaking hands left and right.

DISSOLVE TO:

Later in the evening. Nearing the conclusion of a sumptuous
four-course meal, the party assembled around a banquet table,
a steady murmur of chatter filling the room.

ANGLE ON TOMMY AND SANDRA

As a WAITER pours them more champagne.

                          TOMMY
            So who's the chief conspirator behind
            all this anyway?

                          SANDRA
            Who do you think?

Their eyes fall on TOMMY'S FATHER across the table, a
dignified middle-aged man in a tweed suit and glasses, smiling
with quiet pride.

                          SANDRA
            He's the ringleader, I just helped
            organize.

                          TOMMY
            Why didn't you invite Steve?

                          SANDRA (a bit evasive)
            I dunno...seemed like a family affair
            to be honest...didn't think it was my
            place...

Tommy rolls his eyes, a knowing smile.

                          SANDRA
            What?

                    TOMMY
              (after a beat)
        My parents hardly know the guy, you
        know that. That's the whole point.
        I mean...next to you, he's the best
        friend I have. You have to start
        accepting that.

                    SANDRA
        I do accept that...I just don't trust
        him.

                    TOMMY
              (an old story between them)
        Look, let's not start, tonight of all
        nights. All I'm saying is, he would've
        loved to be here. I mean, the guy's on
        student aid, Sandra.

She falls silent, eyes downcast. Tommy's cousin JOEL
interrupts, passing behind them.

                    JOEL
        Happy birthday, bud.

                    TOMMY
        Hey, thanks. Good luck on the LSAT.

Joel crosses his fingers and disappears as Tommy turns back to
Sandra. He softens to an apologetic tone:

                    TOMMY
        Look, I'm sorry...it's no big deal...
        Just do me a favor, ok? Keep tonight
        under your hat. If he finds out he
        missed a chance to mingle with Dad
        and company, I'll never hear the end
        of it.

She meets his eyes, a faint smile, as Tommy's father CHIMES
his wine glass with a desert fork. Rises to convey a few words:

                    FATHER
        Ladies and gentlemen...Thought I'd do
        this now, before I turn into Andy Capp...
              (warm laughter)
        I'd like to begin by wishing my son --
        my only son -- a very happy 21st
        birthday.

Applause. Tommy shyly rubbing his brow, a bit embarrassed.

9

                    FATHER (solemn now)
        21 has proven to be a seminal year in
        this family's history. My father, God
        rest his soul, began a proud tradition
        at 21...by overcoming very modest roots
        and becoming the first Greene to study
        law at Harvard University.
                (more applause)
        Thirty years later, in Dad's honor, I
        followed. And now I stand before you
        Tommy, on the crest of your 21st
        birthday, with every confidence you're
        going to continue a very proud legacy...
        imminent exception duly noted.
                (scattered chuckles)
        That's right, as many of you know,
        Tommy has set his career sights on
        something "loftier" than the county
        DA's office, which dad and I faithfully
        served for almost a half century. No,
        Tommy has chosen the Justice Department
        as his Holy Grail. He wants to
        prosecute big game some day, and I
        guess teach his old man a few tricks
        in the process...
                (more quiet laughter)
        But seriously folks, all levity aside...
        I'm very proud of this young man and
        what he's set out to achieve. I'd like
        to end by reading a short passage I
        discovered the other day...which I feel
        defines perfectly who our Tommy is...
                (reads from a small note)
        There's a man...and one day he looks up
        to the Lord and cries: There's so much
        pain and evil in the world, God. Why
        don't you send help? And the Lord
        replies: I did send help...

        I sent you.

He looks into his son's eyes.

                    FATHER
        I know you won't let Him down, Tommy.

CLOSE ON TOMMY

Genuinely moved. A heartfelt smile. Indeed the story of his
life -- wanting to make a positive difference, to be somebody.

He nods his thanks to everyone, on the verge of tears, as
applause fills the room.

INT. TOMMY'S HONDA (MOVING) - NIGHT

Tommy is driving, eyes fixed on the road, seemingly deep in
thought. Sandra sits next to him, the sleepy humming of the
wheels the only sound. Finally she breaks the hush:

                    SANDRA
          Did you like the champagne?

Tommy nods quietly.

                    SANDRA
          Really sneaks up on you doesn't it.
          Three drinks and...Jeez-Louise...

She looks to Tommy for a reaction, but he's in another world,
something weighing on his mind.

                    SANDRA
          You ok?

                    TOMMY (after a beat)
          I spoke to Carol Lieberman tonight.
               (off Sandra's look)
          That lady at the bar.

                    SANDRA
          In the black dress.

                    TOMMY (nods)
          She's a good friend of Dad's. She works
          at the Harvard Placement Office.
               (beat)
          Turns out, the Justice Department in
          Washington hires three summer interns
          every year from Harvard Law. First-year
          students.
               (looks at Sandra)
          Carol's in charge of selection. She
          promised me a position.

His words hang in the air for a moment. Sandra speechless.
From her expression, we can see this is a monumental
development.

                    SANDRA
          If you get into Harvard.

He nods.

                    SANDRA
          That's amazing, Tommy! This is your
          dream come true. Why didn't you tell
          me?

11

                    TOMMY (shrugs)
          Because until I get in it's just that:
          a dream.

                    SANDRA
          Don't be ridiculous. Your resume's
          untouchable, sweetie; you got 4.0 GPA--

                    TOMMY
          Sandra, everybody who applies to
          Harvard has great portfolio.

                    SANDRA
          I said <u>untouchable</u>, Tommy. Yours is
          untouchable...
               (beat)
          ...and so are you. Keep it that way
          and you're in.

CLOSE ON TOMMY

Staring tensely at the road ahead. A mountain of pressure on
his shoulders.

EXT. NORTHEASTERN UNIVERSITY - MAIN CAMPUS - NIGHT

Tommy's car rounds a bend and pulls up in front of Sandra's
dorm building.

INT. TOMMY'S HONDA - NIGHT

                    SANDRA
          You sure you don't wanna come in?

                    TOMMY
          Naw, too much work to do.

                    SANDRA (sexy voice)
          I'll give you a birthday backrub.

                    TOMMY (smiles)
          Rain check...

He kisses her: a sweet, soft kiss. She leans into him,
returning his love.

                    SANDRA
          You're gonna marry me some day y'know.

                    TOMMY
          You think so, eh?

                    SANDRA
          I do.

> TOMMY
> ...get outta here already...

They share a smile and she steps out of the car.

> SANDRA
> I love you.

> TOMMY
> Love you too.

INT. TOMMY AND STEVE'S DORM ROOM - NIGHT

A clock radio reads 2:26am. Tommy sits in the glow of his desk lamp, alone in the room, staring at his English Lit midterm. Burning a hole in the "C".

Above his desk, pinned to a bulletin board, are dozens of news clippings: A NY Times piece detailing U.S. Attorney Giuliani's crackdown on insider trading; a front-page article on the prosecution of an international heroin ring; an old Time magazine cover of Robert Kennedy; several more. In fact, every clipping on the board depicts a famous graduate of Harvard Law. High-profile prosecutors. Visionaries. Heroes.

Tommy leans back in his chair and takes a deep breath, eyes shut, wrestling with his conscience.

The SOUND of some keys, and Steve lets himself in, visibly bushed, dressed in bartender attire. They exchange cursory nods and Steve crashes on his bed.

> TOMMY (quietly)
> Long night?

> STEVE (exhales)
> Stan booked early...had to work the
> whole bar alone...

Tommy sympathetically shakes his head, eyes returning to his midterm. A short silence. And he tosses the exam on his desk and rises. He has come to a decision.

He crosses to Steve's side and meets his friend's eyes, allowing himself a final moment's pause, before uttering:

> TOMMY
> Let's talk.

INT. SCHOOL HALLWAY - NORTHEASTERN - DAY

A THRONG OF STUDENTS pour out of a classroom into the hallway, signalling the end of a period, and join a swelling flow of traffic.

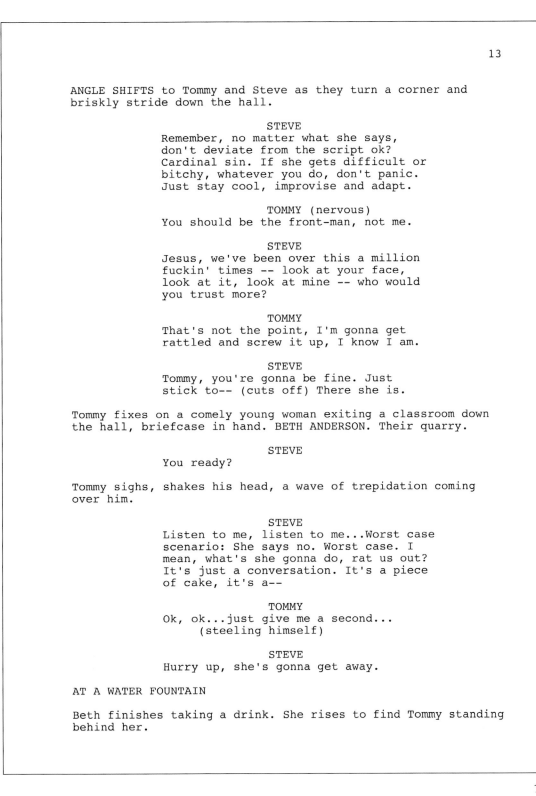

ANGLE SHIFTS to Tommy and Steve as they turn a corner and briskly stride down the hall.

> STEVE
> Remember, no matter what she says, don't deviate from the script ok? Cardinal sin. If she gets difficult or bitchy, whatever you do, don't panic. Just stay cool, improvise and adapt.

> TOMMY (nervous)
> You should be the front-man, not me.

> STEVE
> Jesus, we've been over this a million fuckin' times -- look at your face, look at it, look at mine -- who would you trust more?

> TOMMY
> That's not the point, I'm gonna get rattled and screw it up, I know I am.

> STEVE
> Tommy, you're gonna be fine. Just stick to-- (cuts off) There she is.

Tommy fixes on a comely young woman exiting a classroom down the hall, briefcase in hand. BETH ANDERSON. Their quarry.

> STEVE
> You ready?

Tommy sighs, shakes his head, a wave of trepidation coming over him.

> STEVE
> Listen to me, listen to me...Worst case scenario: She says no. Worst case. I mean, what's she gonna do, rat us out? It's just a conversation. It's a piece of cake, it's a--

> TOMMY
> Ok, ok...just give me a second...
> (steeling himself)

> STEVE
> Hurry up, she's gonna get away.

AT A WATER FOUNTAIN

Beth finishes taking a drink. She rises to find Tommy standing behind her.

                        TOMMY
            Beth Anderson?

                    BETH
        Yes...

                        TOMMY
            Hi, I'm Tommy Greene.

INT. VACANT CLASSROOM - DAY

Tommy leads Beth from a BUSY CORRIDOR into the small room,
where they find Steve waiting, perched on a desk.

                        TOMMY
            This is my buddy, Steve Fox.

                        STEVE
            How's it goin'.

She returns a curt nod.

                        TOMMY
            Take a seat.

He shuts the door to give them some privacy, and a trace of
suspicion crosses Beth's face.

                    BETH
            What's this all about?

                        TOMMY
            Please...? Won't take a moment.

Reluctantly, she pulls up a chair and they all sit down, Tommy
taking the seat directly facing her. Steve removes a pack of
Trident from his pocket.

                    STEVE
        Gum?

                    BETH
        No thanks.

He pops a stick in his mouth and sits back, almost signalling
Tommy to begin. Tommy breaks into a warm, disarming smile to
diffuse the tension (especially his) and leans forward, his
voice sincere and businesslike:

                        TOMMY
            Ok, here's the story...We're both in
            our senior year. Honors English.

He removes two sheets from a folder and slides them to Beth.

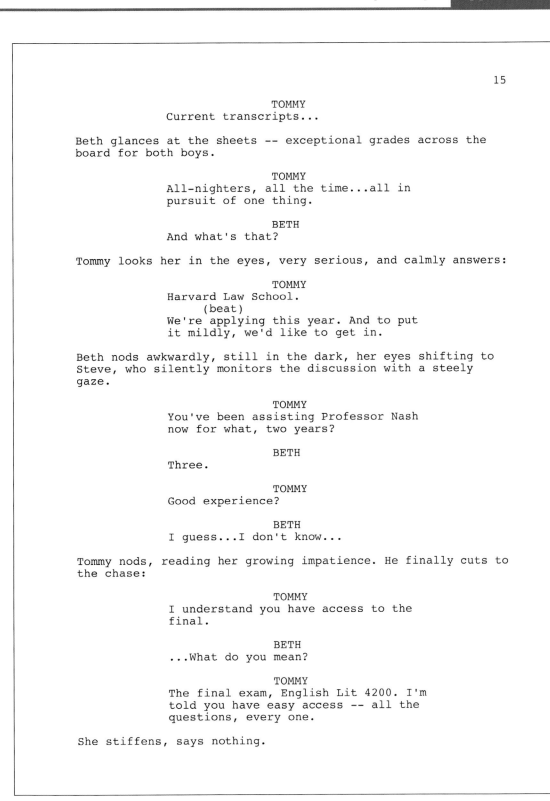

15

                              TOMMY
                    Current transcripts...

Beth glances at the sheets -- exceptional grades across the
board for both boys.

                              TOMMY
                    All-nighters, all the time...all in
                    pursuit of one thing.

                              BETH
                    And what's that?

Tommy looks her in the eyes, very serious, and calmly answers:

                              TOMMY
                    Harvard Law School.
                         (beat)
                    We're applying this year. And to put
                    it mildly, we'd like to get in.

Beth nods awkwardly, still in the dark, her eyes shifting to
Steve, who silently monitors the discussion with a steely
gaze.

                              TOMMY
                    You've been assisting Professor Nash
                    now for what, two years?

                              BETH
                    Three.

                              TOMMY
                    Good experience?

                              BETH
                    I guess...I don't know...

Tommy nods, reading her growing impatience. He finally cuts to
the chase:

                              TOMMY
                    I understand you have access to the
                    final.

                              BETH
                    ...What do you mean?

                              TOMMY
                    The final exam, English Lit 4200. I'm
                    told you have easy access -- all the
                    questions, every one.

She stiffens, says nothing.

                    TOMMY
          Correct me if I'm wrong.

                    BETH
          I don't know what you're talking about.

                    TOMMY
          We know about Margaret Sousa.

                    BETH (defensively)
          Who's Margaret Sousa?

                    TOMMY (soothing tone)
          We're not here to blow the whistle on
          you, I promise. Just a business
          proposal.

She rises, indicating the meeting is over.

                    BETH
          I think you guys have the wrong girl.

Impatience finally overcoming him, Steve stands and interjects
with a cool, measured tone:

                    STEVE
          Look, Margaret Sousa says she paid you
          three grand for a copy of the English
          Lit final two years ago. Now whether
          or not you remember, acknowledge or
          admit it, we really don't give a shit.
          What we <u>do</u> care about are two things:
          Can you still get it, and will you
          accept the same to turn it over?

A silence. Beth quietly processing what she's just heard,
considering the boys, their proposition...Before she can
respond, Tommy adds further inducement, with just the right
shade of humility:

                    TOMMY
          We got "C"s on the midterm, Beth. If we
          don't ace the final, our chances for
          Harvard are slim and none. And slim's
          out of town.

She cracks a faint smile, continuing to percolate impassively,
averting eye contact with the boys.

                    TOMMY
          Will you help us?

Another long beat. <u>And she sits down.</u>

                        BETH
          Two conditions...

                        STEVE
               (takes his seat, pumped)
          Name 'em.

                        BETH
          I want cash -- full amount due on
          delivery.

                        STEVE
          Done.

                        BETH (pauses)
          And I can't let you see the exam until
          the day before you write.

                        TOMMY
          ...Why?

                        BETH
          I can't have it floating around. This
          way you don't have time to distribute
          or sell it.

                        TOMMY
          Beth, we're not gonna do that.

                        STEVE
          We need more time.

                        BETH
          Look, I did the same thing with
          Margaret. Just photocopy somebody's
          class notes, and have your textbook
          handy. I give you the questions; all
          you do is reference the answers and
          memorize them on the spot. Won't take
          you more than a few hours.

The boys share a dubious look.

                        BETH
          It's non-negotiable.

                        STEVE (after a beat)
          Can you confirm you have the exam <u>in
          your hands</u> at least a week before?

                        BETH
          I can do that.

                         STEVE
          Seriously. Seven days -- minimum.

                         BETH
          It's no problem. He prepares it on his
          laptop at least two weeks before. I
          have the password -- easy access
          anytime I want.

                         TOMMY
          What if he changes the password?

                         BETH
          He changes it every week.
               (off their looks)
          Don't worry, it goes from his son's
          name, to his wife, to his daughter,
          then back around again. It's a joke.

Steve looks to Tommy and smiles reassuringly. Tommy takes a
deep breath, not so confident.

                         STEVE
          You got a deal.

                         BETH
          Great.
               (she rises)
          I have to get to class. Here's my
          number. Call me later and we'll work
          out the details.

                         STEVE (as she exits)
          Not bad, Anderson -- five minutes work,
          three grand. Partners at Cravath don't
          haul in that much.

                         BETH
          It's not my time you're paying for.

                         TOMMY
          What are we paying for?

                         BETH (pauses, smiles)
          My cooperation.

And she walks out. Tommy staring after her, uneasy, perhaps
wondering what he's gotten himself into...

FADE TO BLACK. TITLE CARD UP:

          Three Weeks Later
          Commencement of Final Exams

19

INT. TOMMY AND STEVE'S DORM ROOM - NIGHT

For the truly ambitious, a pressure-cooker season of sleepless
nights, twisted backs, and debilitating stress.

Tommy sits at his desk, hunched over some books, studying
hard. Tense, twitching eyes devouring information, his pen
quickly scrawling key terms, passages.

SLOWLY MOVING across the room, we find Steve at his desk in
identical form, beads of perspiration collecting on his
forehead.

The phone RINGS suddenly! Steve SNATCHES the receiver.

                    STEVE (quiet, icy)
          Hello...Yeah...What's the verdict?...

A long silence as he listens. Tommy lifts his head.

                    STEVE (continuing)
          Any backup?...Better make a hard copy
          asap, just in case...Right...Sounds
          good...Ok, later.

He hangs up. Pauses.

                    STEVE
          She got it.

                    TOMMY
          Any problems?

                    STEVE
          Zero. Next Sunday, two o'clock.

Tommy smiles, relieved. Returns to his studies.

INT. STUDENT CENTER - NEXT SUNDAY - DAY

AN ATM coughs out a wad of cash for Tommy. He hands the bills
to Steve who slips them in an envelope. Smirks.

                    STEVE
          If you ain't cheatin', you ain't
          tryin'.

                    TOMMY
          F. Lee Bailey.

                    STEVE
          Give the man a cigar.

They exit.

EXT. STUDENT GHETTO - SIDE STREET - DAY

In high spirits, the boys traverse a low-income neighbourhood
of student apartments and frat houses on their way to Beth's.

                    STEVE
          All those other schools, smack 'em
          together and coat 'em in chocolate,
          still amount to dogshit. I mean, you
          can wander through the Australian
          Outback and they've heard of Harvard.

                    TOMMY
          Mystique from pole to pole.

                    STEVE
          Fuckin-A -- and a red carpet to fame,
          fortune, and a Ferrari 456.

                    TOMMY (chuckles)
          Noble goals to be sure.

                    STEVE
          Yeah, well, "nobility arises from
          sated desire." Laurence Pope.

                    TOMMY
          What a load of crap.

                    STEVE
          Truth hurts.

                    TOMMY
          "Nobility forsakes extravagance, and
          saves the world one case at a time."
          Thomas Greene Sr.

                    STEVE
          King of the Hypocrites.

                    TOMMY
          I'll be sure to tell him that when
          you're looking for a reference.

Without warning, Steve SOCKS Tommy in the shoulder and
retreats a few steps, a grin from ear to ear.

                    STEVE
          You asked for it...

                    TOMMY
          I'm definitely telling 'em now.

And Steve chases Tommy around a corner out of sight, their
howls of laughter fading in the frosty air.

EXT. BETH'S SORORITY HOUSE - DAY

Tommy and Steve appear from behind a brownstone, still
scuffling, and fix on the house.

Their stomachs sink.

TWO POLICE CRUISERS are parked out front, and a knot of
STUDENTS hover around the front steps.

A sharp gust of impending doom cuts through the boys.

ON THE FRONT STEPS

Tommy and Steve penetrate the mob, eyes searching for an
explanation. Off to the side, a couple of sorority sisters can
be seen sobbing, their friends offering support.

>   TOMMY
>   What happened?

>   NEARBY STUDENT
>   Robbery, I guess.

>   STEVE
>   When?

The student shrugs. The boys push forward into:

INT. FOYER - DAY

And spot Beth in the adjoining living room, conferring with an
OFFICER and two friends. She looks pale and distressed.

Steve signals her and she meets his gaze. She heaves a deep
sigh, mutters a few words to her friends, and wearily heads
into the foyer.

>   BETH
>   Outside.

EXT. SIDE OF THE HOUSE - DAY

Tommy and Steve follow Beth to a small, private alcove.

>   STEVE
>   What the hell is goin' on?

>   BETH (terse, nervous)
>   We had a party Friday night, some
>   stuff got ripped off, alright?

>   TOMMY
>   But it's Sunday.

                    BETH
          No shit.

                    STEVE
          You're just discovering it now?

                    BETH
          Look, I don't have time for this, I
          have to get back in there...

                    STEVE
          Fine, where's the exam, we'll get
          outta your way.

Beth exhales and hangs her head. Softly mutters the deathblow:

                    BETH
          ...it's gone.

Silent shock swallows the boys.

                    TOMMY
          What do you mean it's gone.

                    BETH
          ...It's gone. They stole it.

A long pause. The boys just standing there, mouths agape.

                    STEVE
          Why would they steal the exam?

                    BETH (growing more agitated)
          They weren't looking for the fucking
          exam -- they stole my laptop! -- the
          disk with the exam was in the carrying
          case.

                    TOMMY
          You didn't make a backup?

No response.

                    STEVE (heatedly)
          Jesus Christ, Beth, I told you to make
          a hard copy!

                    BETH
          I was going to, I forgot!

And she bursts into tears, sobbing uncontrollably. Tommy
quickly lays a hand on her shoulder, dousing the fire.

                    TOMMY
          Ok, it's ok...

23

> BETH
> (through the tears)
> I'm sorry...they stole all my jewellery
> too...I-I don't have insurance...

> TOMMY
> (nightmare still sinking in)
> Jesus...
> (thinks hard)
> What about the questions, do you
> remember any questions...?

Beth shakes her head, trying to compose herself.

> BETH
> I'm sorry...I hardly looked at it...
> I'm so sorry...

Steve struggling to stay cool, to understand the situation.

> STEVE
> Beth...How could <u>anyone</u> steal all this
> stuff in the middle of a fucking party
> and not be seen?

She shakes off the question and steps away, wiping her tears.

> BETH
> I have to go back in...

> STEVE
> Hold it, wait a minute...Beth...
> please...listen to me...
> (grappling to stay calm)
> I'm sorry about the robbery, I really
> am...But the exam is <u>tomorrow morning</u>.

> TOMMY
> We can't drop the course, Beth. It's
> too late.

> STEVE
> And we haven't studied <u>a fuckin' word</u>!

> BETH (tears returning)
> There's nothing I can do, he's gone
> home for the holidays, he took his
> laptop with him.

> STEVE
> There must be a way.

                              BETH
          There's not.

                              STEVE (grabs her shoulders)
          There has to be a way.

                              BETH (freaks out)
          GET YOUR HANDS OFF ME!

                              STEVE
          Ok, ok, Jesus...

Beth drifts away from the boys, tears streaming down her face,
whimpering:

                              BETH
          I'm sorry...I really am...there's
          nothing I can do...I'm sorry...

And she disappears behind the house, leaving Tommy and Steve
paralyzed in her wake.

A long silence.

INT. TOMMY AND STEVE'S DORM ROOM - DAY

The boys sit on their beds like zombies. Silent. Numb. Eyes
piercing empty space. Mid-afternoon sun filtering in through
the drapes.

Tommy's face in particular reads, I knew something like this
was going to happen. The Harvard poster ironically pinned over
his head, almost mocking him.

A long beat...and Steve rises suddenly, moving to his desk
with new purpose. He pulls out a notebook and starts writing.

Still queasy, Tommy watches his friend for a moment.

                              TOMMY
          What are you doing?

                              STEVE
          PMI.

                              TOMMY
          ...What?

                              STEVE
          PMI. You gonna help me or not?

Tommy pulls himself up and shuffles to Steve. Steve hands him
a pen and paper.

25

                    STEVE
          Plus-Minus-Interesting. Write down
          every feasible option we have, with
          detailed pros and cons. We'll evaluate
          each one, and make a call.

Tommy considers Steve for a moment...slowly building a second
wind...

                    STEVE
          The clock's tickin'.

Tommy nods, and shifts into gear.

A SERIES OF FAST CUTS

As the boys write with intense concentration, pens furiously
scratching paper, forming and reshaping ideas, strategies,
hands crumpling paper...

After several minutes, they're ready to talk.

A score of fast-paced information is thrown on the table:

                    STEVE
          Ok, one thing right off the bat: Any
          option that doesn't promise an "A"
          isn't an option. Agreed?

                    TOMMY
          Agreed.

                    STEVE
          I mean, a shit grade and we can
          forget about--

                    TOMMY
          You're preaching to the converted. I
          don't need convincing.

                    STEVE
          Ok, from the top...

A PEN UNDERLINES - CRAM

                    STEVE
          Fuck it. There's no time, we're not
          prepared.

                    TOMMY (nods)
          Best case scenario, C-plus.

                    STEVE
          With crib sheets and a horseshoe up
          the ass maybe.

"CRAM" IS CROSSED OUT.

> TOMMY
> Let's face it: Writing tomorrow isn't
> an option under any circumstance.

> STEVE
> Unless we get a copy of the final
> beforehand.

> TOMMY
> We tried that -- that's how we got
> here.

<u>EXTENSION</u> IS UNDERLINED.

> TOMMY
> This is by far our best bet -- I mean,
> as far as I'm concerned there <u>are</u> no
> other options. Postpone it for two
> weeks and study our asses off.

> STEVE
> Postpone it how?

<u>FAMILY CRISES</u> IS CIRCLED.

> TOMMY
> Could be anything -- death in the
> family, some serious illness...Only in
> this case, it'd be somebody we both
> know.

> STEVE
> What about proof?

PAGES FLIP BEFORE OUR EYES -- A Northeastern publication
titled <u>Academic Policies and Procedures</u>.

And a finger runs down to the heading <u>Final Examinations</u>.

> TOMMY (reading)
> ...In all cases, students will be
> required to provide <u>formal verification</u>
> of the emergency circumstance.

> STEVE
> I told ya.

> TOMMY
> I can't believe it. Your mom bites the
> dust and they ask to see the fucking
> coffin.

                    STEVE
Let's move on.

                    TOMMY
Keep that one on standby. What else?

DOCTOR'S NOTE IS CIRCLED.

                    TOMMY
Listen to this: I know a guy who went
to Health Services last year and told
the doctor he OD'd on caffeine pills
cramming for his midterm. Said his
vision was blurred and he couldn't
read anything. Got an extension until
the following week.

                    STEVE
        (another problem dawning on him)
Oh Christ...

                    TOMMY
What?

                    STEVE
We're overlooking a glaring fuckin'
conflict here.
        (off Tommy's look)
Think about it: If we formally tell the
school we're out of commission for two
weeks, we can't write our other exams.
        (Tommy hangs his head)
Fuck, I have three this week alone. I
don't wanna postpone those, I'm ready
now.

Frustrated, Tommy crumples his notes and pitches them across
the room.

                    STEVE
All these options are fraught with
fucking disaster anyway. I mean, take
a doctor's note: We both have to lie
to an MD, pray he doesn't call our
bluff, and even if he does give us a
note, we have to risk fraud against
the school and reschedule our other
exams. And for all that, we're still
not guaranteed shit. If I risk my ass
there better be gold at the finish line.

Tommy doesn't say a word, eyes to the floor.

A long silence.

                    TOMMY
        We have to call Beth...there's no other
        way. We have to call her, calm her down,
        and <u>beg her</u> to go to Nash's. I mean,
        Jesus, the answer to our prayers is
        sitting right there in his damn house.

                    STEVE
        Beth's a dead end.

                    TOMMY
        That's defeatist.

                    STEVE
        She'll <u>never</u> <u>fucking</u> <u>do</u> <u>it</u>.

                    TOMMY (exasperated)
        You got any better suggestions?

Another stretch of silence, this time HOLDING ON STEVE...his
dark, piercing eyes...on the verge of proposing what's been at
the back of his mind since they started.

                    STEVE
        ...I say we get the exam ourselves.

ON TOMMY

Both puzzled and incredulous, eyes reading Steve for any hint
of a jest.

                    STEVE
        I'm serious as a heart attack.
            (beat)
        We practically have the password...

Tommy's expression wrought with disbelief.

                    STEVE
        Seriously, it's a cinch to look up.

Eyes adding, What do you think?

An uncomfortable silence...and we CUT TO:

INT. HALLWAY OUTSIDE BOYS' DORM ROOM - DAY

We faintly hear their VOICES behind the door, heated,
bickering, growing louder. Suddenly, the door SLAMS OPEN, and
Tommy pushes past Steve.

                    STEVE (hisses)
        For chrissakes, where's the harm in
        checking it out?

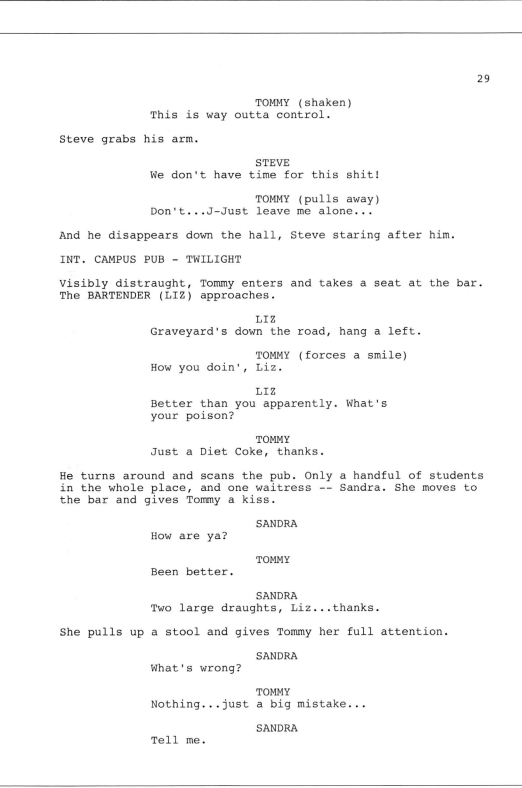

29

                         TOMMY (shaken)
              This is way outta control.

Steve grabs his arm.

                         STEVE
              We don't have time for this shit!

                         TOMMY (pulls away)
              Don't...J-Just leave me alone...

And he disappears down the hall, Steve staring after him.

INT. CAMPUS PUB - TWILIGHT

Visibly distraught, Tommy enters and takes a seat at the bar.
The BARTENDER (LIZ) approaches.

                         LIZ
              Graveyard's down the road, hang a left.

                         TOMMY (forces a smile)
              How you doin', Liz.

                         LIZ
              Better than you apparently. What's
              your poison?

                         TOMMY
              Just a Diet Coke, thanks.

He turns around and scans the pub. Only a handful of students
in the whole place, and one waitress -- Sandra. She moves to
the bar and gives Tommy a kiss.

                         SANDRA
              How are ya?

                         TOMMY
              Been better.

                         SANDRA
              Two large draughts, Liz...thanks.

She pulls up a stool and gives Tommy her full attention.

                         SANDRA
              What's wrong?

                         TOMMY
              Nothing...just a big mistake...

                         SANDRA
              Tell me.

                         TOMMY
                 (sighs, looks her in the eyes)
            Let me put it this way...I ain't
            untouchable...

A short silence, Sandra growing more concerned.

                         SANDRA
            What've you done?

                         TOMMY
            Just forget it.

                         SANDRA
            What do you mean forget it, are you in
            trouble? What did you do?

                         TOMMY
            Sandra...please, not now...

She issues a sigh of resignation as Liz places two beers on
her tray.

                         SANDRA
            Be right back.

He watches her leave, eyes falling on a figure entering the
bar, rushing toward him. Steve.

                         TOMMY
            I don't wanna hear it.

                         STEVE
            Just shut up and listen...I got the
            password.
                 (off Tommy's look)
            His wife's name is Joan, son Richard,
            daughter Heidi -- it's right there
            in his bio in the course calendar.
            And listen to this: I called his
            house. No answer.

                         TOMMY
            You used our phone?

                         STEVE
            I called from a pay phone. Look, he
            lives out in Landover. Closest
            neighbor on either side is probably
            like a hundred yards away.

Tommy shakes his head; he knows where Steve is heading.

                         STEVE
            Just drive me out there--

31

                    TOMMY
          No.

                         STEVE
          I promise, I'll do everything. I'd
          take your car myself, but I can't drive
          stick. <u>I'm just asking for a ride</u>.

They lock eyes as Sandra returns and flicks Steve a stony
glance.

                         SANDRA
          Steve.

                         STEVE
          Sandra.

                         SANDRA
          What's going on?

                         STEVE (to Tommy)
          Every minute counts.

Tommy broods a moment longer...and rises.

                         TOMMY (to Sandra)
          I have to go.

                         SANDRA
          Where are you going?

                         TOMMY
          Tell you later...
               (meets her eyes)
          I promise.

And he hurries out behind Steve. HOLDING on Sandra...

EXT. HIGHWAY - NIGHT

Tommy's Honda STREAKS across a desolate rural landscape,
bathed in the glow of a full moon.

                         TOMMY (V.O.)
          Try him again, we're almost there.

The SOUND of a cell phone being removed from its cradle.

                         TOMMY (V.O.)
          Block the call.

                         STEVE (V.O.)
          What is it, *-6-9?

> TOMMY (V.O.)
> *-6-7, then the number.

The SOUND of an electronic dial. Some ringing...and Nash's voice mail picks up.

> STEVE (V.O.)
> Still no answer.

INT. HONDA - NIGHT

CLOSE ON dashboard clock -- 11:42pm. The car now parked on a dirt road fringing a dark patch of woods.

Tommy sits alone in complete silence, waiting, knots in his stomach, his breath misting the windshield.

He hears rapidly approaching FOOTSTEPS. Braces himself.

It's Steve -- He quickly slips into the car and whispers:

> STEVE
> I think Lady Luck just gave us a
> blowjob.

> TOMMY
> What?

> STEVE
> There's no security system, I'm
> positive, I checked the whole
> perimeter. And there's a small
> basement window at the back I know
> I can force open.

He digs through a gym bag in the back seat and hands Tommy a penlight.

> STEVE
> Here.

> TOMMY
> What's this?

> STEVE
> I need your help.

> TOMMY
> No way.

> STEVE
> I can't do it otherwise -- I can't
> open the window without you.

33

                        TOMMY
            I knew it, I knew you were gonna do
            this.

                        STEVE
            Do what! For fuck's sake, I'm tryin' to
            save your ass too! Nobody's home! It's
            a fuckin' cakewalk!

                        TOMMY
            You <u>think</u> nobody's home.

                        STEVE
            No lights on, no cars in the garage,
            nobody answers the phone.

                        TOMMY
            Did you knock?

                        STEVE
            No.

                        TOMMY
            Then you don't know shit.

                        STEVE
            I'm goin' in one way or another,
            asshead. Why the hell would I risk
            waking somebody up?

Tommy heaves a sigh. Steve's patience at an end.

                        STEVE
            Are you gonna help me or not? Yes
            or no.

TIGHTENING to Tommy...

EXT. PROFESSOR NASH'S HOUSE - NIGHT

The moon hangs low and baleful over an old, restored farm
house. A thin layer of frost on the ground.

ANGLE ON BACKYARD

Completely surrounded by a dark forest.

Suddenly, in the distance, Tommy and Steve emerge from the
woods like two black phantoms, silent, barely visible against
the shadowy trees. Staying low to the ground, they creep
across the yard toward the house.

AT THE SOUTH WALL

The boys squat before the small basement window. It's about 2'x 2', hinges on one side, and opens INTO the house, locked shut by a flimsy interior latch.

Steve sits on the ground and positions the heel of his shoe on the window frame. Whispers to Tommy:

> STEVE
> Hold it tight.

Tommy manages a shaky grasp on the window with both hands, and Steve begins to push with his shoe, CAREFULLY, applying controlled, increasing pressure...Tommy tightly holding the frame, ensuring the window doesn't suddenly slam open...

Finally, a faint, muffled CRACK. The boys freeze. Exchange glances. Tommy releases his grip.

Steve rolls to his hands and knees and easily PUSHES THE WINDOW OPEN. Tommy exhales.

INT. BASEMENT - NIGHT

Pitch black except for the dull glow from the window. The boys peering in on a small, empty laundry room.

Tommy holds the window open as Steve slides in, feet momentarily coming to rest on a clothes dryer directly beneath the window before reaching the floor. He turns to Tommy and signals, Come on. Tommy shakes his head, No way.

Steve flashes his penlight beam in Tommy's face and mouths: "I need your help!" Again, Tommy vehemently shakes his head. Steve presses: "It's gonna take me a fuckin' hour to do it alone!" and before we know it they're engaged in a ridiculous argument, hurling silent obscenities back and forth, faces twisted in anger. Steve finally cools off and appeals to Tommy with one final word: Please.

A long beat...and Tommy succumbs. He enters in the same fashion as Steve, but makes considerably more NOISE, giving them both mild panic attacks.

Finally, they both stand on the damp concrete floor. And begin to search the house for Nash's laptop.

A SERIES OF SHOTS

As the boys prowl the dark basement from room to room, tiny penlight beams dancing, playing off walls, tables, etc. Finding nothing.

The GROUND LEVEL is next:

INT. KITCHEN - NIGHT

The boys rise into view from the basement, eyes scanning every corner, every countertop. As they slip into the living room, something catches Tommy's eye:

A PULSE OF RED LIGHT on the wall near the fridge. Tommy stops in his tracks. Focuses on the light -- a small, soft flash every second. It appears to be an alarm system. He begins to approach, slowly, cautiously, as it continues to pulse. It seems to be emanating from a small rectangular unit. Tommy trains his penlight beam on the unit and discovers:

A TELEPHONE. The flashing light is the "Messages Waiting" indicator, and the LCD display reads: <u>Ringer is OFF</u>.

Tommy spins around to warn Steve, but it's too late; Steve has disappeared into the living room.

INT. LIVING ROOM - NIGHT

Tommy enters and tries to flag Steve down, but Steve is already across the room, scouting the foyer with his back to Tommy.

Almost immediately, something breaks the silence -- a SOUND... very faint...coming from an upstairs bedroom. <u>The boys freeze</u>. Listen hard...

The sound is unmistakable -- SNORING -- muted, but definitely real.

Tommy frantically waves to Steve, shaking his head, pointing back toward the basement. But Steve ignores him and continues to search the ground floor.

Nerves on a wire edge, Tommy backs into a tall ceramic lamp, nearly knocking it over -- its shadow tottering back and forth, before he snatches and secures it. He releases a quivering breath.

Steve, meanwhile, has reached the foot of the stairs leading to the upper level. There's no question where he wants to go. He looks at Tommy. Tommy shakes his head, <u>Please no!</u>

Steve glares, and starts up the stairs anyway. Tommy stands firm, holding his position in the living room. He backs into a dark corner, out of sight.

STEVE
Stealthily climbs the stairs, hand gliding over the wood bannister, the SNORING growing louder and louder.

TOMMY
Shuts his eyes, fists clenched, mouthing a short prayer.

STEVE
Reaches the upper floor. Two bedrooms. One occupied by
PROFESSOR NASH (source of the snoring). The other, empty.

Moving down the hall he spots a bathroom next, and then:
A STUDY. Even draped in shadows, there's no mistaking it. He
enters.

TOMMY'S PRAYER
Is suddenly interrupted. His eyes SNAP OPEN and his breathing
stops. He's sure he just heard something. His eyes DART to the
left...and a light TURNS ON around the corner.

He goes stiff as a board. Heart starting to POUND, awaiting
his doom. Suddenly, a figure appears in a nightrobe -- Nash's
teenage DAUGHTER -- emerging from a bedroom the boys missed.
She walks right past Tommy and starts up the stairs toward the
bathroom.

IN THE STUDY
Steve kneels before a large desk and fixes on a LAPTOP.
Elated, he silently opens it. Turns down the volume dial.
Flips it on.

NASH'S DAUGHTER
Continuing up the stairs, almost at the top.

TOMMY
Petrified. On the verge of a nervous breakdown.

STEVE'S EYES
Gleaming in the dark, glued to the screen as the computer
boots up. Suddenly, he hears the floor CREAK outside his door.
He DUCKS out of sight.

NASH'S DAUGHTER
Enters the bathroom, casting a quick, disinterested glance
toward the study -- the door is half closed (blocking the glow
of the computer screen). She shuts the bathroom door and goes
about her business.

TOMMY AND STEVE - SEPARATE SHOTS
Paralyzed. Waiting for what seems like an eternity. Eyes
glazed with fear.

OUTSIDE THE BATHROOM DOOR
We hear a FLUSH, which triggers:

INT. NASH'S BEDROOM
Nash to wake up.

HIS DAUGHTER
Exits the bathroom, COUGHING quietly, and proceeds back
downstairs.

37

TOMMY AND STEVE - SEPARATE SHOTS
Still listening on pins and needles...

NASH'S DAUGHTER
Reaches the ground floor, passes Tommy, and returns to her
bedroom. Her light turns off. Tommy exhales.

INT. NASH'S BEDROOM
Nash sits up, the SOUND of the toilet receding.

STEVE
Assuming the coast is clear, creeps back to the laptop and
fixes on the screen. A password is requested. He silently
types in J-O-A-N and presses Enter.

Password not accepted.

He types H-E-I-D-I next...and stops. Did he hear something
outside the door?

CUT TO:

NASH
Now standing in the hall only ten feet from the study, eyes
rivetted to the half-closed door. All he has to do is push it
open and it's all over.

But he doesn't. Instead, he turns and starts down the stairs.

TOMMY
Hears Nash descending, but

STEVE
Doesn't. He presses Enter. Again, not accepted. He types in
the final option: R-I-C-H-A-R-D. Not accepted.

Panic is starting to set in now. He shuts his eyes and
composes himself for a moment, then takes a final stab with
D-I-C-K. Punches Enter.

A Windows Program Manager lights up the screen.

Steve exhales. He's in.

NASH
Reaches the ground level, passes Tommy, missing him by an
armslength, and proceeds to his daughter's bedroom.

STEVE
Scans the various program options -- E-mail, Excel, CorelDraw,
etc. Double clicks on MS Word.

TOMMY
Listens as Nash checks on his daughter, their VOICES a faint
murmur:

                              NASH (O.S.)
                  Is everything ok, honey?

                              DAUGHTER (O.S.)
                  I still feel nauseous...

Her bedroom light flips on again.

STEVE
Scrolling down a list of file names, opening anything that
might be the exam, striking out every time.

TOMMY
A pair of eyes in the darkness, hanging on every word that
drifts from the young girl's bedroom.

STEVE
Reaching the bottom of the list, his options almost exhausted.
Finally, he spots a file name that makes his eyes go wide:
EL4200. He double clicks.

TOMMY
Stiffens as the bedroom light flips off, signalling Nash's
imminent return.

STEVE
Has hit the jackpot. The English Lit. final exam flickers
across the screen. He quickly removes a diskette from his
pocket, inserts it in the disk drive, and copies the file.

NASH'S SHADOWY FIGURE
Appears from around the corner. He's heading back to his
bedroom. Tommy praying Steve stays hidden.

STEVE
Quickly removes the diskette, slips it in his pocket, closes
the laptop and silently exits the room.

TOMMY'S EYES
Following Nash as he glides by toward the stairway...

And in a heart-stopping moment, Tommy finds himself in the
most terrifying situation of his life:

Steve starting down the stairs / Nash starting up the stairs.

Tommy's eyes wide as silver dollars, heart in his throat...

Suddenly, a VOICE punctures the terror -- Nash's daughter
calling her father:

                              DAUGHTER (O.S.)
                  Daddy...

Nash stops at the foot of the stairs and turns back, leaving Steve stunned and frozen at the top.

He quickly slips back into the study, hides behind the door.

TOMMY
Holding his breath. Perfectly still.

                    NASH (O.S.)
          What is it, honey?

                    DAUGHTER (O.S.)
          Leave the bathroom light on please?

                    NASH (O.S.)
          I will. Good night, sweetheart.

Nash climbs the stairs, turns on the bathroom light, and returns to his bedroom.

TOMMY AND STEVE - SEPARATE SHOTS
Hearts racing. As relieved as they can be. Tommy shuts his eyes.

EXT. NASH'S HOUSE - AN HOUR LATER - NIGHT

The boys silently emerge from the basement window, close it, exchange glances and...

SPRINT LIKE BLACK PANTHERS across the yard, vanishing into the woods.

HOLLYWOOD

PRODUCTION _____

DIRECTOR _____

CAMERA _____

DATE   SCENE   TAKE
_____   _____   _____

Index

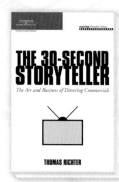
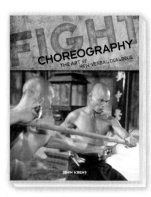

License Agreement/Notice of Limited Warranty

By opening the sealed disc container in this book, you agree to the following terms and conditions. If, upon reading the following license agreement and notice of limited warranty, you cannot agree to the terms and conditions set forth, return the unused book with unopened disc to the place where you purchased it for a refund.

License:

The enclosed software is copyrighted by the copyright holder(s) indicated on the software disc. You are licensed to copy the software onto a single computer for use by a single user and to a backup disc. You may not reproduce, make copies, or distribute copies or rent or lease the software in whole or in part, except with written permission of the copyright holder(s). You may transfer the enclosed disc only together with this license, and only if you destroy all other copies of the software and the transferee agrees to the terms of the license. You may not decompile, reverse assemble, or reverse engineer the software.

Notice of Limited Warranty:

The enclosed disc is warranted by Course Technology to be free of physical defects in materials and workmanship for a period of sixty (60) days from end user's purchase of the book/disc combination. During the sixty-day term of the limited warranty, Course Technology will provide a replacement disc upon the return of a defective disc.

Limited Liability:

THE SOLE REMEDY FOR BREACH OF THIS LIMITED WARRANTY SHALL CONSIST ENTIRELY OF REPLACEMENT OF THE DEFECTIVE DISC. IN NO EVENT SHALL COURSE TECHNOLOGY OR THE AUTHOR BE LIABLE FOR ANY OTHER DAMAGES, INCLUDING LOSS OR CORRUPTION OF DATA, CHANGES IN THE FUNCTIONAL CHARACTERISTICS OF THE HARDWARE OR OPERATING SYSTEM, DELETERIOUS INTERACTION WITH OTHER SOFTWARE, OR ANY OTHER SPECIAL, INCIDENTAL, OR CONSEQUENTIAL DAMAGES THAT MAY ARISE, EVEN IF COURSE TECHNOLOGY AND/OR THE AUTHOR HAS PREVIOUSLY BEEN NOTIFIED THAT THE POSSIBILITY OF SUCH DAMAGES EXISTS.

Disclaimer of Warranties:

COURSE TECHNOLOGY AND THE AUTHOR SPECIFICALLY DISCLAIM ANY AND ALL OTHER WARRANTIES, EITHER EXPRESS OR IMPLIED, INCLUDING WARRANTIES OF MERCHANTABILITY, SUITABILITY TO A PARTICULAR TASK OR PURPOSE, OR FREEDOM FROM ERRORS. SOME STATES DO NOT ALLOW FOR EXCLUSION OF IMPLIED WARRANTIES OR LIMITATION OF INCIDENTAL OR CONSEQUENTIAL DAMAGES, SO THESE LIMITATIONS MIGHT NOT APPLY TO YOU.

Other:

This Agreement is governed by the laws of the State of Massachusetts without regard to choice of law principles. The United Convention of Contracts for the International Sale of Goods is specifically disclaimed. This Agreement constitutes the entire agreement between you and Course Technology regarding use of the software.